LIVE LIFE
DELICIOUSLY

TARATEASPOON

LIVE LIFE
DELICIOUSLY

RECIPES FOR BUSY WEEKDAYS
& LEISURELY WEEKENDS

TARA BENCH

SHADOW
MOUNTAIN

Photography by Ty Mecham
Prop Styling by Veronica Olson

Visit us at shadowmountain.com

Library of Congress Cataloging-in-Publication Data

Names: Bench, Tara, author.
Title: Live life deliciously : recipes for busy weekdays & leisurely weekends / Tara Bench.
Description: [Salt Lake City] : Shadow Mountain, [2020] | Includes index. | Summary: "Tara Bench shares some of her best-loved recipes to inspire home chefs to elevate their easy weeknight meals as well as prepare elegant party dishes for weekend gatherings"—Provided by publisher.
Identifiers: LCCN 2020013021 | ISBN 9781629727851 (hardback)
Subjects: LCSH: Cooking, American. | LCGFT: Cookbooks.
Classification: LCC TX715 .B46575 2020 | DDC 641.5973—dc23
LC record available at https://lccn.loc.gov/2020013021

Printed in China
RR Donnelley, Dongguan, China

10   9   8   7   6   5   4   3   2   1

FOR MY MOM—THANK YOU
FOR TEACHING ME TO COOK
AND TO SHARE FOOD WITH
LOVE AND ENJOYMENT.

CONTENTS

INTRODUCTION

THE CHAPTERS AT WORK

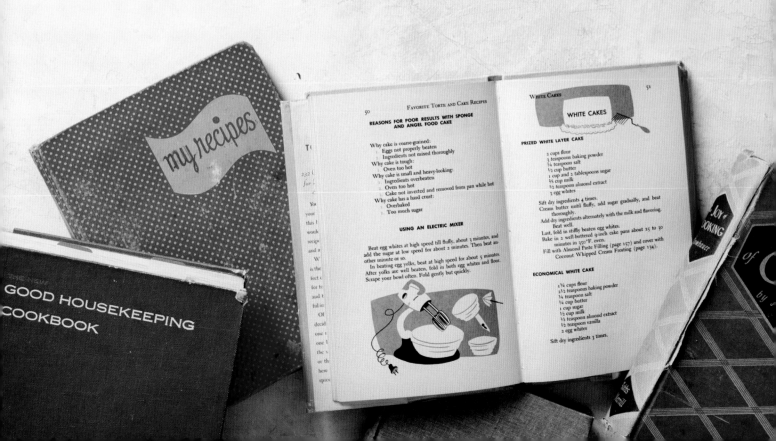

INTRODUCTION

THERE IS ALTOGETHER too much cooking goodness in the world to pack into one cookbook. Every season of every year we get to revel in the delicious bounty around us and figure out new ways to eat the seasonal colors and offerings.

This goodness is yours when you reach for that extra spice or new ingredient and bring people together to share it. To me, there's nothing better than splendidly nourishing yourself, your friends, and your family. Here is where I can be with you in the kitchen and inspire you to *live life deliciously.*

It's impossible to narrow my favorite techniques, meals, flavors, tips, and treats into one book, let alone share all of the things I've learned along the way while working shoulder to shoulder with some of the best in the food business. I've been cooking professionally for more than twenty years, sharing classic, new, and innovative recipes on TV and in magazines, books, and online. I feel so lucky to have been able to immerse myself in something I love as my profession.

I grew up in the kitchen and don't remember a time when I wasn't by my mom's side as she cooked. I was the girl with the Easy-Bake Oven, and I graduated to real kitchen equipment when I was quite young. I'd do any task Mom gave me. She is an excellent cook and was always a patient teacher. By her side, I learned to knead bread dough until the gluten had formed properly, handle pastry crust, stir a cheese sauce to perfection, make family meals, and graciously entertain.

Out of college, I landed an internship in the test kitchen of *Martha Stewart Living.* I learned a million more things about food and cooking. I learned recipe development, food styling, and publishing. I worked alongside the lifestyle industry's most talented creators, art directors, and photographers. It was an invaluable experience.

I worked my way from intern to senior food editor in a handful of years and watched the company grow and change. I cherish the experience and the work I did there, and I still love thumbing through old issues to reference the recipes I was able to produce on those pages.

A few years after leaving *Martha Stewart Living*, I became the food director of *Ladies' Home Journal* magazine. It was one of the first women's magazines ever published and has an enchanting 130-year legacy of teaching women to cook. As an editor there, I created recipes for everyday and mainstream lifestyles. I loved the challenge of coming up with dishes that were innovative and inspiring, but also easy and accessible.

I now develop recipes and produce food content for brands, companies, and various magazines, as well as write my blog. I appear on TV, lifestyle shows, and online videos, sharing delicious food and my tips for cooking. I get to cook and eat for a living! I couldn't ask for a more ideal job.

Here I share recipes you can enjoy and make over and over again. So much of our life is digital these days, including my website TaraTeaspoon.com, but this book is something tangible that can be a companion to you in the kitchen and something I hope you'll make notes in and love.

Whatever your routine or schedule, take time, and add new skills, new recipes, and new flavors to your life. Cook, and enjoy your time in the kitchen. I invite you to bring people together around the table and make memories, whether it's a weeknight or a leisurely weekend.

THE CHAPTERS AT WORK

I BELIEVE A COOKBOOK is both a record and a starting place. Once I write a recipe, I tend to change and revise it, turning it into something else. Perhaps that is why so many of the recipes in this book are used as parts of other recipes.

I'm a collector of cookbooks—especially vintage and family collections—and relish these records of personality, culture, and history. I have a little of that feeling here as a tribute to my cooking heritage. I've made a career out of styling food and making it look amazing, but food isn't always made to impress people. It's also about nourishing and bringing comfort into homes. Whether the food looks good, tastes good, or both, eating it together is the best way to really connect with people.

I encourage you to use this book as a starting point, then a guide, then as inspiration for your own cooking. Here's a walk through the chapters and what you can expect.

Any casual or fancy gathering is made better with food! In BITES, DIPS, AND SNACKS you'll find irresistible nibbles, snacks to have in your repertoire, and my cheese board makeover. (I'll give you a hint: butter!)

SALADS, BOWLS, AND DRESSINGS can truly make a meal. Whether it's a main course salad or one served on the side, there's something wonderful about a bowl full of chopped, sliced, diced and shredded food—all tossed together in tasty bliss. The dressings and vinaigrettes are meant to be used interchangeably. Make a complete meal with any of these salads by adding a protein such as chicken, beef, shrimp, or tofu. Even a spoonful of beans or chickpeas gives a salad a hearty boost.

Being on the sidelines is just as important as being the main event in my book. The chapter SIDE LOVE is filled with those veggie, starchy, and cheesy moments that make a meal complete. Small touches like browning butter for green beans and arranging potatoes artfully in the baking dish only take a few extra minutes, but make these recipes phenomenal in their supporting roles.

WEEKNIGHT ROUTINES—Whether it's a tasty meatball recipe, a versatile seasoning rub, or a savory chicken marinade, these recipes can inspire creativity. Every two recipes uses one flavor-boosting recipe, or a leftover protein to inspire two weeknight dinners. Once you master the common recipe, you can come up with your own meal ideas. The purpose is to share simple ways to make weeknight cooking easier, more dynamic, and diverse.

The recipes in FLAVOR-INSPIRED DINNERS are recipes I love and that I go back to time and time again. Some are inspired by the delightful dinners I've enjoyed at restaurants in New York City, while others are from my travels around the world or takes on family favorites. These are globally inspired, flavorful recipes to explore in your own kitchen.

My passion is feeding people, and I love gathering friends and family in the kitchen. MEALS FOR GATHERING are for these moments, when you are entertaining or just creating a great Sunday dinner. These elegant entrees and nourishing comfort foods are meant to feed a crowd and make a heart happy.

MORNING GLORIES are the tastiest way to start the day. From my grandmother's pancakes to a Spanish tortilla you may have never tried, I hope you find a favorite that starts new family memories.

I could have written an entire book on SWEETS TO SHARE. Sugary goodness is my weakness, and making desserts is my favorite way to procrastinate and relax. I make more friends with baked goods so why not make it the biggest chapter? Sweets are meant to be devoured with company. Come one, come all!

NEW PANTRY STAPLES

⸺•⸺

THE RIGHT EQUIPMENT

NEW PANTRY STAPLES

I MAY BE introducing you to some new flavors in this book. I've listed my favorite seasonings, spices, sauces, and ingredients that set up what I call "the new pantry staples." Some of these foods may not have been in your cupboard several years ago, and now are more commonplace, helping you create amazing everyday meals and delightful dishes for entertaining. Some of the new flavors are from other countries and cultures and are a blend of regional and traditional favorites that make up our modern way of eating.

Adding these items to your pantry, freezer, or spice rack will make your cooking easier and more flavorful. Stocking up on these basics means you can focus on fresh produce, meat, and dairy during your trips to the store. Stock up and start cooking!

Apricot jam

Artichoke hearts—frozen or canned

Bacon

Baking powder

Baking soda

Breadcrumbs—regular and panko

Broth—chicken or vegetable

Butter—unsalted

Capers

Canned beans—chickpeas, white beans, black beans

Chocolate—dark and milk

Cocoa powder, unsweetened

Coconut milk

Cornmeal

Cornstarch

Fish sauce

Flour

Garlic

Ginger—fresh

Golden raisins

Honey

Hot sauce

Lemons

Limes

Molasses

Nuts—almonds, pecans, walnuts, pine nuts, hazelnuts (store in the freezer)

Olive oil—extra-virgin and regular

Onions—red, yellow, and shallots

Parmesan

Pasta—orecchiette, large shells,
    noodles, lasagna, orzo

Red curry paste

Rice—long grain and short sushi

Roasted red peppers

Salsa—red and salsa verde (jarred)

Salt—kosher salt, flaked sea salt

Sesame oil

Soy sauce and ponzu

SPICES
- Cayenne
- Chili powder
- Cinnamon
- Coriander
- Cumin
- Dry mustard
- Garlic powder
- Oregano
- Paprika—sweet and smoked

SPICES (continued)
- Peppercorns
- Red pepper flakes
- Sesame seeds
- Sumac
- Thyme
- Turmeric

Sugars—white and brown

Sweet chili sauce

Tahini

Tomato paste

Vanilla

Vegetable oil

Vinegars—balsamic, white balsamic,
    red wine, sherry, rice wine,
    apple cider

Yogurt—plain and vanilla

THE RIGHT EQUIPMENT

FOR MANY YEARS I enjoyed going to work in spacious, well-designed magazine test kitchens, with every tool imaginable readily available. At home, I kept my specialty cooking needs to a minimum. When I left the magazine world, I had to fit all of my tools into a tiny New York City kitchen the size of a bathroom. You think I'm kidding. Go stand in your bathroom and imagine making Thanksgiving dinner in a kitchen that size. I've done it!

I resorted to storing specialty pans and extra gadgets in bins in my closet; I stashed my salad spinner under my bed!

I now have what you'd call a medium-sized, New York City kitchen and have strategically fit everything in it—even if my pots and pans are hanging from pegboards on the walls.

For me, enjoying time in the kitchen begins with having the right supplies and equipment. You don't have to have a decked-out, chef-style kitchen to be equipped; there is a way to make even the smallest kitchens work.

Having used and tested countless pans, tools, gadgets, and small appliances over the years, I have a passion for what works best. Here I've boiled it down to the best of the basics—the must-haves in my opinion. This "essentials" list is lengthy, and I don't expect you'll attain everything all at once. I do find cooking is more enjoyable when I don't have to improvise with tools or wash a pan to use it again when I'm in a hurry. With these tools, you'll have everything you really need to make cooking fun and feel like you can try any recipe in this book!

POTS AND SAUCEPANS

Invest in quality pots and saucepans. For everyday cookware, quality means looking for stainless steel tri-ply pans with an aluminum core. Aluminum provides even heat distribution; stainless steel on the outside prevents aluminum from leeching into your food and also makes for easy cleanup. I highly recommend pans with tri-ply thickness all the way up the sides, not just in a plate on the bottom. This protects sauces and custards from scorching on the thin sides of a pan.

A useful kitchen will include a small 2-quart saucepan for melting or browning butter, a medium 3- to 4-quart saucepan (great for simmering, reducing, making custard, and cheese sauce), and a 6- to 8-quart large pot. I highly recommend the large pot be an enameled cast iron, like Le Creuset. It's an investment, but it cooks evenly and is perfect for heavy searing, simmering, and braising. I use it for my pot roasts, curries, soups, and more.

For other stockpots and soup pots larger than six to eight quarts, there is no need to invest in tri-ply technology. Larger pots are great for boiling potatoes or pasta.

I recommend getting stainless steel as your basics, and if you add on with nonstick pots later, it's a nice bonus. I find nonstick saucepans aren't as durable with all the stirring and whisking I do in them.

SKILLETS AND NONSTICK TECHNOLOGY

I'm a huge fan of having several different kinds and sizes of skillets on hand. Stainless steel or nonstick skillets are great, though make sure all the handles are oven-proof in case you need to finish the cooking in the oven.

One of my favorites is a high-sided sauté pan for cooking large portions of vegetables or making one-pot meals. The larger surface area is perfect for searing, quick-cooking veggies, and wilting spinach, and can accommodate extra ingredient add-ins and sauce.

A 10- to 12-inch sloped-sided skillet is a great everyday pan, nice for delicate jobs like omelets or crêpes, and for Spanish tortillas and hash browns. Both nonstick and a well-seasoned cast-iron skillet are great choices.

Stock a small, nonstick 6-inch skillet for toasting a grilled cheese, frying tostadas, or scrambling an egg.

I like to have a mix of tri-ply stainless steel skillets—which are great for getting a crispy sear on meat and making flavorful pan sauces—and nonstick skillets for clean cooking and easy cleanup.

A quality stainless steel skillet can last for decades with proper care, and thus justifies a greater investment. You don't need to invest in expensive nonstick skillets. Even high-end nonstick skillets that incur normal wear and tear will scratch and need to be recycled within a year or two. (Nonstick pans that incur heavy use typically last only a year.)

No one wants to throw an expensive pan in the trash every twelve months! Instead, look for PFOA-free Teflon or ceramic-coated nonstick cookware, and don't spend a lot.

PFOA-free Teflon skillets are perfectly healthy to cook on until they become scratched and overly used. Ceramic-coated skillets do not pose any health risks with scratching, but they do lose some of their nonstick qualities over time. A thin layer of silicone over the ceramic coating makes them extra slippery at first, but this layer can wear off in time. When this happens, you'll need a bit of butter to help your omelet or other delicate foods release.

KNIVES

My passion runs deep for a good knife! Good, sharp knives are one of the most important tools in a kitchen. They make for quick and efficient cutting, chopping, and slicing, which truly makes cooking more fun.

I could spend an entire chapter on knives, but I'll keep it simple: I recommend high carbon stainless steel knives. All steel alloys include carbon and iron, but an alloy with higher carbon creates a superior knife that is easy to sharpen and holds its edge well. I prefer forged knives for their strength and durability, rather than stamped or pressed knives, but I have some of both!

You can buy knives online or in the store, but I recommend going to a store and feeling different knives in your hand before buying. A knife should feel comfortable. You'll be surprised at how different the brands and sizes feel in your hand and how a knife that feels comfortable to one person might not to another. (Remember to hold a chef's knife correctly, up on the bolster, not down on the handle. Ask the knife purveyor for more details or check out my page on knives on TaraTeaspoon.com.)

An 8-inch chef's knife is a must-have in every kitchen. To that, I'd add a 6-inch chef's knife, a slicing knife, a paring knife, and a serrated knife.

If you want a few fun extras in your knife drawer (or block), try a 6-inch utility knife (both serrated and straight), a Santoku knife, a serrated paring knife, and a double serrated knife.

CUTTING BOARDS

Having the right cutting board is one of the best ways to protect the knives you've invested in! Chopping and cutting on glass boards, composite boards with lots of hard glues, or hard plastic boards can damage and dull your knives. I like to have soft plastic and rubber cutting boards on hand in all sizes. They are easy on knife blades and a breeze to clean (and bleach if you cut raw meat on them). I often throw them in the dishwasher for cleanup.

Wood cutting boards are also great for knives and preferred by many chefs, but they can't be put in the dishwasher and must be regularly maintained with oil.

TONGS

Tongs are an extension of your hand! I have long ones for reaching into deep pots or across sizzling skillets, medium tongs for tossing salads and turning or removing my veggies from their pans, and tiny tongs for tossing, stirring, and picking up small ingredients from the skillet. I recommend getting a pair in each size.

MIXING BOWLS

Mixing bowls are one kitchen tool you need a lot of. Fortunately, they nest easily and don't take up too much space. I recommend having a set of glass, stainless steel, and plastic mixing bowls. Each set should have at least four bowls in varying sizes. Glass mixing bowls are great when you need to microwave something you're stirring. Stainless steel bowls are typically wider and deeper, which means you're less likely to spatter the ingredients everywhere when mixing cakes or whipping cream. Plastic or melamine bowls work well for whisking up dressings, stirring together ingredients, and holding prepared mixtures.

SPATULAS

Like mixing bowls, spatulas are another kitchen item you'll want to have around in spades. I have a lot of spatulas, and I use all of them.

Silicone spatulas, also known as rubber scrapers or rubber spatulas, are a mainstay in my kitchen. I use them for stirring, scraping sauces and batters out of pans and bowls, and more. Don't be afraid to have five or six in your kitchen—in varying sizes. No one wants to stop to wash their one rubber scraper three different times for one recipe!

Standard spatulas, or pancake turners as many call them, are used for turning and flipping food! It's nice to have a plastic one to use on your nonstick skillets and griddles and a metal one for removing delicate cookies from a baking sheet.

Small, offset spatulas, with narrow metal blades, are my favorite cooking tool. A friend once counted twenty-four of these in my kitchen. I use them to frost cakes and cupcakes and to spread anything on everything! In fact, I'm more likely to reach for one of these to make a peanut butter sandwich than I am a butter knife. The offset shape makes this tool great for spreading and it fits right in my hand.

STAND MIXER

There are lots of brands and styles to choose from, but if you make bread and dough a lot, I'd recommend a Bosch. You also can't go wrong with the tried-and-true KitchenAid. I particularly like the metal bowl because I can set it over a pot of simmering water to melt things, throw it in the fridge to chill, and then pop it in the dishwasher for easy cleanup. That hand mixer will only get you so far.

BLENDER

Some preparations simply can't be made without a blender. But while it's nice to have a powerful version like a Vitamix or Blendtec, a standard Hamilton Beach or Oster blender will almost always do the trick.

FOOD PROCESSOR

This is the small appliance most often left out of a kitchen. I've found that people think of a food processor as a luxury item and wait to invest. Don't wait! I find a food processor as important in a kitchen as standard pots and pans, and dishwasher-safe models means cleanup is a breeze.

A 9- or 11-cup model is your best bet for most recipes. I swear by my Cuisinart, but any brand will do for everyday jobs.

MANUAL CITRUS SQUEEZER

A simple, manual citrus squeezer will make cooking more pleasant whenever a recipe calls for freshly squeezed citrus juice. With these tools, there's no juice spraying all over and no seeds slipping into your bowl.

They also yield a lot more juice from of a piece of fruit than a traditional reamer. Just cut the fruit in half, plop it in the juicer, and pull down the lever to juice! If manual squeezers aren't your thing, a small countertop reamer will also do the trick.

MICROPLANE GRATER

Please have a fine Microplane grater in your kitchen! It's a must for citrus zest. I also love it for mincing garlic cloves, grating whole nutmeg, and shaving Parmesan.

BOX GRATER

A box grater is imperative for grating zucchini, carrots, and apples into those perfect little shreds. It's also ideal for grating cold butter, hard cheeses, dry breadcrumbs, and other things.

The grater plate on your food processor will give you the same result, but, unless I'm grating a lot of cheese or vegetables, I like to pull out a hand held box grater.

BAKING SHEETS

In professional kitchens, an 18-by-13-inch rimmed baking sheet is called a half-sheet pan. I recommend having several half-sheet pans on hand. They work well for baking cookies and rolls, roasting vegetables, and baking sheet cakes.

If you want to add some baking sheets to your supply, rimmed quarter-sheet pans—which are half the size of a half-sheet pan—are one of my favorites to use when making smaller batches of cookies or roasted veggies. They can even sub for a 9-by-13-inch pan when making brownies.

It's also nice to have a couple of baking sheets without rims. I prefer higher-gauge stainless steel baking sheets to flimsy aluminum sheets. I can slide a sheet of parchment paper filled with baked cookies right off the edge of an un-rimmed baking sheet without ruining them!

9-BY-13-INCH PANS

A 9-by-13-inch ceramic or tempered-glass pan (think Pyrex), is a mainstay for casseroles. I also like to have a few metal pans of the same size on hand. Metal pans don't have the intense sloped sides and corners that glass pans do, so they create a nice-shaped cake. They are also great for roasting a small chicken or making a sheet-pan dinner for two!

PARCHMENT PAPER

Parchment paper is your best tool for creating a nonstick surface on baking pans. You can even make packets out of parchment and fill them with chicken or fish to cook in the oven. I prefer to buy my parchment online in flat, pre-cut sheets. You can keep a roll on hand if you prefer. I just don't like fighting with the curls when I'm laying the paper in a pan.

MISE EN PLACE BOWLS

Mise en place is a French cooking term that means having everything in its place. You *mise en place* before starting to cook a recipe to ensure you have all the ingredients prepared and ready to use. Any little bowls will help you do this. I love them for holding bits of ingredients, melted butter, spice mixtures for a rub or cake, and sprinkles and dragées when I'm decorating cakes or cookies. These little bowls can be glass, ceramic, plastic, or metal; whatever the material, it's nice to have a stack of them handy in any kitchen.

BITES, DIPS, AND SNACKS

parmesan and herb white bean dip

THIS RECIPE IS so versatile. It's creamy, savory, and delicious. Glorious as a dip or a sandwich spread (New York Focaccia Sandwich, page 169), this dip is also perfect on crostini or bruschetta. Serve with veggies, breadsticks, crackers, and charcuterie.

I use the same technique for this dip as I do for my ultra-smooth hummus found on my blog. Simmering the already cooked canned beans with baking soda makes the skins extra soft, so when blended, your dip is smooth and luscious. There's no metallic aftertaste because you'll rinse away the baking soda water. I promise the results are worth the extra step.

MAKES

3 CUPS

HANDS-ON TIME

25 MINUTES

TOTAL TIME

25 MINUTES

2 (15-ounce) cans cannellini (white kidney) beans

1 teaspoon baking soda

2 small cloves garlic

1 tablespoon fresh lemon juice

¼ to ½ teaspoon kosher salt

½ teaspoon ground coriander

2 tablespoons extra-virgin olive oil, plus more for top

½ cup finely grated Parmesan

2 teaspoons thyme leaves

⅓ to ½ cup boiling water

Flat-leaf parsley and coriander seeds, for garnish

Dippers, such as crackers, crostini, endive leaves, sweet peppers, and other vegetables

TARA'S TIP

Use a fine-mesh sieve instead of a colander when draining the cooked beans. The large holes of a colander will let too many of the soft bean bits escape down the sink.

1. Pour beans with their canned liquid into a medium saucepan. Cover with water to ½-inch above the beans. Add the baking soda. Bring to a gentle simmer, and simmer for two minutes. This will take 8 to 10 minutes total. Drain in a fine sieve and rinse in hot water.

2. While beans cook, in a food processor or blender combine the garlic, lemon juice, ¼ teaspoon salt, coriander, and olive oil. Pulse and then let sit until the beans have finished cooking.

3. Add the drained beans, Parmesan, and thyme, to the food processor and blend until smooth, scraping the bowl as needed. Drizzle ⅓ cup hot water while the machine is running and let process until desired, smooth consistency is achieved.

4. Add salt and more boiling water to reach the taste and texture you desire. Garnish with parsley, crushed coriander seeds, and olive oil, if desired. Serve warm or at room temperature for the best taste. May also be served cold. Dip can be refrigerated for up to one week.

MAKES

6 TO 8 SERVINGS

HANDS-ON TIME

15 MINUTES

TOTAL TIME

20 MINUTES

burrata with grilled peaches and orange zest chimichurri

I COULD EAT burrata with anything, or nothing, anytime, anywhere, and always adore it. I encourage you to make it part of your regular routine!

Burrata is made of fresh mozzarella gently wrapped around a filling of soft curd and cream. Quite heavenly when you slice into it and take a bite.

The sweet and tangy flavor of the peaches intensifies with time on the grill, and my pistachio chimichurri is a divine accompaniment. Place it on top of burrata-slathered grilled bread and enjoy!

1 recipe Pistachio and Orange Chimichurri (page 81), prepared

6 to 8 (6-inch) bamboo skewers, soaked in water 20 minutes

3 freestone peaches, washed and cut into 8 wedges each

Extra-virgin olive oil

2 (12- to 16-ounces) balls fresh burrata cheese

1 loaf rustic bread, sliced, brushed with olive oil, and grilled

1. Heat grill to medium-high. Thread 2 or 3 peach slices onto each skewer and lay on a plate or baking sheet. Brush with a little olive oil.
2. Grill peaches, gently turning once, until marked on both sides and just warm. Alternatively, grill indoors on a grill pan or under the broiler.
3. Arrange grilled peaches on plate with the burrata. Drizzle with olive oil and top with some of the chimichurri. Garnish with extra pistachios and orange zest, if desired. Serve with grilled bread.

LOOKS DELICIOUS Adding fresh orange zest and crushed pistachios as garnish takes the presentation to a beautiful place. That little sprinkle of vibrant freshness is easy and makes the dish look picture perfect.

butter board with baguettes

I REIMAGINED THE CLASSIC cheese board into a butter board. Creamy butter is a blank canvas for whatever you want to mix in or sprinkle on it. And really, isn't a crusty baguette with butter all anyone wants? I do—it's delicious!

A schmear, a swirl, and a spread later, you'll have an appetizer (or a full-on dinner in my case) that everyone will enjoy. These are essentially compound butters—butters with added ingredients—that are often melted on top of steak or dropped into a soup, and they are amazing as a spread for crusty bread.

I highly suggest investing another dollar in extra-creamy European or Irish butter. They are higher in fat content and have a luxurious silkiness and flavor.

MAKES

1 CUP COMPOUND
BUTTER PER RECIPE

HANDS-ON TIME

20 MINUTES

TOTAL TIME

20 MINUTES

GARLIC BASIL BUTTER

1 head garlic

1 tablespoon olive oil

1 cup (2 sticks) unsalted butter, softened

2 tablespoons finely chopped sundried tomatoes packed in oil

4 teaspoons finely chopped basil, plus more for garnish

Maldon sea salt flakes

1. Heat oven to 400°F. Cut just the top off the head of garlic. Place garlic head on a 5-inch square of foil and drizzle with olive oil. Seal the foil around the garlic and bake until soft, about 30 minutes. Cool completely.
2. Squeeze garlic from the papery skins into a medium bowl. Add butter and blend with an electric mixer until incorporated and smooth.
3. Stir in sundried tomatoes and basil.
4. Serve butter, sprinkled with salt flakes and basil.

ROSEMARY OLIVE BUTTER

1 cup (2 sticks) unsalted butter, softened

2 teaspoons finely chopped rosemary, plus more for garnish

1 tablespoon finely chopped kalamata olives, plus more for garnish

Maldon sea salt flakes

1. In a medium bowl, with an electric mixer, blend together butter, rosemary, and olives until incorporated and smooth.
2. Serve butter, sprinkled with salt flakes, extra rosemary, and olives.

TARA'S TIP

I call for unsalted butter, but you can use salted if you'd like, just know everything will taste a little more salty!

You can make the butters in advance and store covered in the fridge up to 3 days. Bring butter just to room temperature to use. Serve with baguette slices or larger pieces of bread that people can tear apart and dip.

LOOKS DELICIOUS Serve one or multiple butters at once to create a beautiful board. I used a #867 open star tip to pipe the butter onto a platter.

HERB AND BLACK PEPPER BUTTER

1 cup (2 sticks) unsalted butter, softened

1 teaspoon ground black pepper, plus more for garnish

1 tablespoon finely chopped chives, plus more for garnish

1½ teaspoons finely chopped thyme, plus more for garnish

1 tablespoon finely chopped flat-leaf parsley, plus more for garnish

Maldon sea salt flakes

1. In a medium bowl, with an electric mixer, blend together butter, pepper, and herbs until incorporated and smooth.
2. Serve butter, sprinkled with salt flakes and extra herbs.

BALSAMIC CARAMELIZED ONION BUTTER

2 tablespoons olive oil

1 medium yellow onion, finely diced

2 teaspoons finely chopped thyme, plus more for garnish

2 tablespoons balsamic vinegar

1 cup (2 sticks) unsalted butter, softened

Maldon sea salt flakes

Cracked black pepper

1. Heat oil in a large skillet over medium-high heat; add onions and cook until onions start to become translucent, about 4 minutes. Add thyme and reduce heat to medium-low. Cook, stirring occasionally, until onions are caramelized and golden brown, about 20 minutes. Stir in balsamic vinegar and cook 2 minutes.
2. Remove from heat and let mixture cool completely.
3. In a medium bowl, with an electric mixer, blend butter with onion mixture just until incorporated and smooth.
4. Serve butter, sprinkled with salt flakes, pepper, and extra thyme.

little italy snack board

THERE ARE TWO Little Italy areas in New York City: the one you are probably familiar with is wedged between Chinatown and Soho downtown while the other Little Italy is on Arthur Avenue in the Bronx. The Manhattan area has been commercialized and diluted somewhat, but you can still find a great plate of pasta there. Arthur Avenue still holds on to some strong and authentic Italian-American roots. Regardless, whether you're wandering those neighborhoods, browsing through a grocery store in nearly any neighborhood, or hitting up the pizza stand in Lidia Bastianich's Eataly, the taste of red tomatoes and the green lusciousness of basil come easy in New York City.

Fortunately, these Italian ingredients are readily accessible across the country, so everyone can enjoy their own Little Italy experience.

MAKES

10 TO 12 SERVINGS

HANDS-ON TIME

40 MINUTES

TOTAL TIME

40 MINUTES

1 package cheese tortellini

Assorted cheeses, such as Moliterno with Truffles, Fontina Val d'Aosta, and Pecorino

1 recipe Marinated Tomato, Artichoke, and Mozzarella (page 33), prepared

1 jar marinara sauce

1 bunch haricot verts or thin green beans, stems trimmed

Assorted cured meats, such as soppressata, salami, and prosciutto

Mixed olives

Pistachios or other nuts

Assorted fruit, such as figs, melons, and grapes

Assorted crostini, breadsticks, and crackers

1 recipe The Ultimate Focaccia (page 31), prepared

Rosemary and thyme sprigs, for garnish

TARA'S TIP

Making a few of your own recipes to go on this snack board is absolutely delicious, but the beauty of these ingredients is that you can assemble something like this from all store-bought items. Mix and match depending on your time and tastes.

1. Prepare tortellini according to package directions. Drain, cover, and set aside.
2. Start with the cheese and arrange pieces on one large board or several boards.
3. Place marinated mozzarella salad, marinara, olives, and nuts in separate, small bowls and arrange around cheese.
4. Fill in board with remaining ingredients, nestling haricot verts, fruit, assorted meats, and crostini, breadsticks, and focaccia between cheese and bowls. Add tortellini last so it doesn't dry out. If desired, garnish with sprigs of thyme and rosemary.

LOOKS DELICIOUS When assembling a board like this, I start with the cheeses and any small bowls I'm using. Set those items on your board first, spacing them out attractively. Add other ingredients one by one, nestling them around the cheese, small bowls, and each other. Before you know it, the board will look luscious and inviting.

the ultimate focaccia

THIS IS THE ULTIMATE FOCACCIA—in my opinion, of course! Versions of this flat-bread vary, depending on the region of Italy and even the surrounding countries where it's made. For me, truly perfect focaccia is soft and lofty with a little chew. An occasional drip of rosemary-infused olive oil oozing into the center doesn't hurt either. It should be thick enough to slice in half for sandwiches (The New York Focaccia Sandwich, page 169), but not so thick the ratio of chewy inside and golden outside is thrown off. I like to use this for sandwiches, snack boards (Little Italy Snack Board, page 29), appetizers, or just on the side of a great Italian meal.

My friend Ayelet introduced me to this no-mixer-needed method of making focaccia. It's a take on Jim Lahey's no-knead bread technique and depends on a stretch-and-fold motion, time, and yeast to work the dough from the inside out. This process activates the gluten naturally by turning sugar into carbon dioxide gas (the bubbles and air in the dough). That's why it's important to treat focaccia dough gently and not mash and knead it with any force, which would push out all the air.

MAKES

2 9-BY-13-INCH
PANS, OR
1 HALF-SHEET PAN

HANDS-ON TIME

45 MINUTES

TOTAL TIME

2 HOURS

½ teaspoon active dry yeast	3 cups room-temperature water
2 teaspoons granulated sugar	Extra-virgin olive oil
2 teaspoons salt	Fresh rosemary
6¾ cups (1 pound, 12 ounces) all-purpose flour, plus extra for dusting	Maldon salt or flake sea salt

1. In a large bowl, mix the yeast, sugar, and salt into the flour. Pour water over the flour mixture and mix with a wooden spoon or your clean hand until well incorporated.

2. Using a plastic dough scraper or rubber spatula, scrape down the sides and bottom of the bowl, mixing until there aren't any clumps of flour remaining, about 2 minutes. (The dough will be very sticky, so you're really just scraping it away from the bowl sides and folding it on top of itself).

3. Cover the bowl with plastic wrap and set it aside in a warm place until dough has risen slightly, about 30 minutes.

4. Drizzle a tablespoon of olive oil around the edges of the dough. Use a dough scraper or your hand to lift one-quarter of the dough from the bottom of the ball and stretch it up and over itself. Do not press down on the dough. Do this for all four sides of the ball of dough.

5. Cover the bowl again with plastic wrap and set it aside for 20 minutes.

6. Repeat the folding of each "side" as in step 4. Cover and let dough rest 20 more minutes. After this rest, the dough will look smoother, and if you pull out a small piece of it, you should be able to stretch it a fair bit before it breaks apart.

7. Heavily flour your work surface. Gently transfer the dough onto the floured surface and generously flour the top of the dough. Gently fold the dough over itself once or twice, stretching a bit as you do. Cover the dough and let it rest for another 20 minutes while you prepare your pan(s).

Don't be afraid to get your hands doughy. The first mix is the messiest, but your hands are the best mixers and can feel if the dough is smooth.

This recipe makes enough to fill a half-sheet pan (or two 9-by-13-inch pans) so you'll have extra for the next day if you aren't making it for a gathering.

8. Cover the bottom of a half-sheet pan (13-by-18 inches) or 2 9-by-13-inch pans with 2 to 3 tablespoons olive oil. If using 2 pans, divide the dough in half. Gently lift and stretch the dough into the pan (or pans), stretching rather than pressing it into the shape of the pan.

9. Loosely cover with plastic wrap and let it rest in a warm spot until it has doubled in size, about 30 minutes, depending on the temperature of your kitchen. Do not over-proof at this stage.

10. While the dough rests, heat the oven to 475°F. Place the oven rack in the lower third of the oven.

11. Use floured fingers to make deep depressions in the dough ½ to 1 inch apart, touching the bottom of the pan. Drizzle ¼ cup olive oil over the dough, and then sprinkle it with some rosemary leaves and sea salt flakes.

12. Bake until the focaccia is nicely browned around the edges and golden brown on top, 11 to 13 minutes. Drizzle the hot focaccia with more olive oil if desired. Serve warm or at room temperature.

LOOKS DELICIOUS This focaccia is simple and beautiful with just rosemary and salt, but feel free to nestle cherry tomatoes into the dough, or sprinkle with sliced red onion or sliced fennel and other herbs before baking. These delicious ingredients add flavor and visual appeal.

marinated tomato, artichoke, and mozzarella

MAKES

3 CUPS

HANDS-ON TIME

10 MINUTES

TOTAL TIME

1 HOUR 10 MINUTES

A QUICK, DOWN AND DIRTY cheese-and-tomato salad is a glorified version of marinated mozzarella, but I just couldn't leave well enough alone. Artichoke hearts take it to the next level. Serve on an Italian snack board, spoon over a green salad, with grilled meats or bread, or toss with cooked, cooled pasta for a picnic pasta salad.

1 (8-ounce) container mozzarella bocconcini, drained

2 tablespoons mixed chopped herbs, such as basil, parsley, or thyme

1 cup multi-color cherry tomatoes, cut in half or quarters

1 (14-ounce) can artichoke hearts (not packed in oil), cut in half or quarters

1 small clove garlic, thinly sliced

¼ cup extra-virgin olive oil

1 teaspoon kosher salt

Pinch red pepper flakes

In a medium bowl, mix together all ingredients and refrigerate, covered, for 20 minutes to 1 hour before serving. Can be refrigerated for up to 4 days.

tulum snack spread

WHEN I VISITED TULUM, MEXICO, my friends and I woke up at 6 a.m. to get tacos at a street stand that sells out before ten in the morning. Those tacos were worth the sleep sacrifice.

I grew up eating my mom's absolutely delicious, yet Americanized, Mexican food. In my teens, we moved to Arizona, and I fell in love with every authentic Mexican restaurant and meal we had.

This snack spread is inspired by a lifetime of eating Mexican, Tex-Mex, and Southwest deliciousness. It is so good, you'll want to make it for a weeknight dinner, not just a party.

I make my baked chips, salsas, and queso the day before to allow the flavors to meld overnight and become even more delicious, then assemble this glorious board the day of my gathering. Assuming you've done the same, it should take you less than an hour to cut cheese, prep guacamole, and assemble your spread using store-bought additions.

HANDS-ON TIME

45 MINUTES

TOTAL TIME

45 MINUTES

1 recipe Restaurant-Style Salsa (page 39), prepared

1 recipe Mango, Pineapple, and Pepper Salsa (page 38), prepared

1 jar salsa verde

1 recipe Tex-Mex Queso Dip (page 37), prepared

1 recipe Ridiculously Delicious Grapefruit Guacamole (page 36), prepared

1 recipe Spicy Oven-Baked Chips (page 38), prepared

1 bag plantain chips

1 bag tortilla chips (mini, corn, or blue corn)

10 ounces Pepper Jack cheese, cubed (about 2 cups)

Roasted pepitas

Baby sweet peppers

Jarred pickled jalapeño slices

Sliced radishes

Hot sauce (I love Cholula or Chipotle Tabasco)

Place each salsa, the queso, and the guacamole in separate bowls and arrange on a board or platters with chips, cheese cubes, and other accompaniments. Serve with hot sauce.

TARA'S TIP

A saucy refried bean dip is a great addition to your Tulum Spread. My "cheat" spicy bean dip is as simple as heating 1 (14-ounce) can of refried beans with ⅓ cup water, ¼ teaspoon kosher salt, and 1 to 2 teaspoons of hot sauce. Serve warm or at room temperature. For an extra flavor bonus, add a 4-ounce can of diced green chilis.

LOOKS DELICIOUS The food does all the work on this snack assembly, touting pretty shaped chips, colorful salsas, and cubed cheese. I like to vary the size of my bowls and boards to add to the beautiful look of this party spread. Choose your bowls and vessels before filling them and practice arranging them so you know you have the look you want.

MAKES

ABOUT 3¼ CUPS

HANDS-ON TIME

15 MINUTES

TOTAL TIME

15 MINUTES

ridiculously delicious grapefruit guacamole

IF YOU'VE NEVER added fruit to your guacamole, now is the time to start! The combo of creamy avocado, lime juice, and spiciness mixed with tangy grapefruit on a salty chip is heaven.

This dip is customizable. If grapefruit isn't in season, swap in chopped grapes; or skip the fruit and add roasted, diced poblano peppers, or fresh diced Anaheim chilis. The secret is the simple avocado base with a magic combo of lime, jalapeños, and onions. You'll be a guacamole master almost immediately with this recipe.

TARA'S TIP

To segment grapefruit, use a knife to cut the peel off and remove all the white pith. Then run a sharp knife on either side of the fruit segments, separating them from the membrane. Work over a bowl and then you can squeeze the leftovers into the bowl to save the juice.

4 large or 5 small, ripe avocados

1 teaspoon kosher salt

3 tablespoons fresh lime juice

2 teaspoons hot sauce, such as Cholula

1 medium jalapeño, seeded and finely chopped

3 scallions, white and green parts finely chopped

1 ruby red grapefruit, peeled, membrane removed, and chopped

½ cup chopped cilantro

1. Pit and peel avocados and gently mash in a medium bowl.
2. Add the salt, lime juice, hot sauce, jalapeños, and scallions and stir until blended to desired consistency—chunky or smooth. Fold in grapefruit pieces and cilantro. Serve immediately.

LOOKS DELICIOUS I use a pastry blender or potato masher to smash the avocados. This creates the perfect texture of creamy and chunky. A large avocado should yield about 1 cup of chopped avocado. If your avocados are on the small side or if the pits are huge, just add an extra half or whole one to get the right amount.

tex-mex queso dip

PICTURE ME, spooning queso dip all over everything. That's really what my food dreams look like, and this boot-clicking, spur-spinning, spicy, melty, cheesy dip makes an appearance often.

I made a few delicious trips to Texas when I had family living there, and I knew I had to recreate my favorite restaurant queso. I added short-cut twists and a unique ingredient: sodium citrate. A necessary addition to create a smooth texture.

Store-bought salsas are my helpful shortcut. They add the developed flavor you need for the base of this dip. However, for an authentic queso, you have to add the remaining layers of flavor on your own by roasting fresh peppers and sautéing garlic.

Finish the dip with a mix of melty American cheese and a really delicious sharp cheddar like Tillamook, which is aged for over nine months to create a glorious, bold, and tangy flavor. It's the perfect touch for a true Tex-Mex creation.

MAKES

3¼ CUPS

HANDS-ON TIME

45 MINUTES

TOTAL TIME

55 MINUTES

1 Anaheim pepper or New Mexico chili

1 tablespoon unsalted butter

2 cloves garlic, minced

¼ cup jarred fire-roasted tomato salsa

½ cup jarred salsa verde

1 tablespoon fresh lime juice

¼ teaspoon kosher salt

1 cup half-and-half

½ teaspoon sodium citrate

10 ounces white or yellow American cheese, cubed (about 2 cups)

2½ ounces shredded sharp white cheddar (¾ cup)

1. Heat broiler to high, with rack 4 to 6 inches from the heating element. On a foil-lined pan, broil the whole chili pepper, turning it occasionally to char it on all sides, about 10 minutes total. Remove chili and let it cool until you can handle it. Peel off skin and remove seeds. Finely chop pepper and set aside with any juices from the cutting board.

2. In a large saucepan over medium-high heat, melt butter. Add garlic and stir 30 seconds. Add roasted tomato salsa and salsa verde, lime juice, salt, and chopped pepper with any juices; cook, stirring frequently, until some of the liquid is reduced, about 2 minutes.

3. Reduce heat to medium-low. Add half-and-half and sodium citrate. Stir in cheese cubes and shredded white cheddar, a little at a time, stirring constantly until cheese is melted, 8 to 10 minutes.

4. Serve immediately or cool and refrigerate in an airtight container up to 2 days.

TARA'S TIP

My favorite queso-loving restaurant in Texas serves the hot, melty cheese over a big spoonful of guacamole in the bottom of the bowl. Topped with hot sauce, cilantro, and cotija and it's almost a meal itself!

To reheat chilled queso, gently warm in the microwave or on the stove until just hot.

LOOKS DELICIOUS Sodium citrate is a natural compound used as an emulsifier. It can be found in some health food stores or online. The queso will still be delicious without it, but it will have a slightly curdled texture.

mango, pineapple, and pepper salsa

MAKES

3 CUPS

HANDS-ON TIME

20 MINUTES

TOTAL TIME

20 MINUTES

A MANGO SALSA is what I'd consider the queen of fruit salsas—deliciously simple yet complex enough to take on the king of the dippers, a tortilla chip. Lime juice and salt bring out the intense, aromatic flavor of mango in a salsa, forgoing the need for your typical tomato. Mango isn't overpowering and plays so well with others. The addition of pineapple makes you feel like you're eating on a beach somewhere. I'll take that, anytime.

1 mango, peeled and diced (¾ cup)	½ large jalapeño, seeded and finely diced
¼ of a pineapple, peeled and diced (1 cup)	½ teaspoon kosher salt
½ yellow bell pepper, diced (⅔ cup)	1 tablespoon fresh lime juice
¼ cup finely diced red onion	⅓ cup chopped cilantro
1 scallion, white and green parts finely chopped	

TARA'S TIP

You can use this salsa for more than a dip. The sweet fruit pairs perfectly with peppers and spice to create a condiment exceptional enough to spoon over grilled fish, steak, or chicken, or serve on tacos and quesadillas.

1. In a medium bowl, stir together the mango, pineapple, bell pepper, onion, scallion, jalapeño, and salt.
2. Just before serving, stir in lime juice and cilantro. Prepared salsa can be stored in the refrigerator in an airtight container for up to 2 days.

LOOKS DELICIOUS I like to dice my mango, pineapple, and bell pepper into roughly the same size (slightly larger than ¼ inch). This makes the salsa look more uniform and appealing. If you make the salsa ahead of time, leave the cilantro out until just before serving to keep it bright and fresh.

spicy oven-baked chips

MAKES

ABOUT 20 LARGE CHIPS

HANDS-ON TIME

10 MINUTES

TOTAL TIME

20 MINUTES

THESE TASTY CHIPS are my version of Mexican crackers. Light, flakey, and oversized, they are perfect for spreading with guac or dipping in salsas. You can already buy a great corn chip, so I opted to make these quite lovely crackers out of flour tortillas, but I will continue to call them chips!

¼ cup olive oil or avocado oil	1 teaspoon ground cumin
1 tablespoon fresh lime juice	½ teaspoon chili powder
2 teaspoons kosher salt	5 flour tortillas

1. Heat oven to 375°F. In a bowl, combine oil, salt, cumin, and chili powder. Brush mixture generously on both sides of each tortilla. Cut tortillas into quarters (or large wedges) and place them in a single layer on 2 baking sheets.
2. Bake, rotating sheets halfway through, until tortillas are light golden and crisp, 6 to 8 minutes. Let cool and serve. Chips can be stored airtight for up to a week.

restaurant-style salsa

MAKES

4 CUPS

HANDS-ON TIME

15 MINUTES

TOTAL TIME

15 MINUTES

THIS SAUCY, authentic salsa is cilantro-heavy with a tomatoey, spicy kick. The original recipe came from my friend Gina by way of my sister Marie. (It's smart to keep salsa-loving people around you in life!) I've made a few tweaks to suit my taste, but I kept the El Pato tomato sauce—a must for packing in flavor without extra work.

El Pato sauce is a simple tomato sauce prepared with chilis, onions, garlic, and spices. The flavors are mellowed and perfect because it's cooked and canned, and it's right there on the store shelf in a yellow can, as handy as can be.

Traditional canned tomato sauce also makes an appearance in this easy salsa. It adds a caramelized, savory-sweet richness that fresh tomatoes don't have. Every brand of tomato sauce will vary slightly in flavor. My friend swears by Hunt's, but I encourage you to find your own favorite. This salsa is really good after it mellows in the fridge for a day, as the flavors get a chance to party together.

1 (15-ounce) can tomato sauce	¾ teaspoon kosher salt
1 (7-ounce) can El Pato tomato sauce	½ teaspoon ground black pepper
1 small bunch cilantro, big stems removed, coarsely chopped (about 1½ cups)	1 teaspoon dried oregano
	1 teaspoon ground cumin
6 small scallions, white and green parts chopped	¼ teaspoon red pepper flakes
	1 cup boiling water
¾ teaspoon garlic powder	

1. In a blender, combine the tomato sauce, El Pato, and all other ingredients except the boiling water and process until pureed.
2. Add the boiling water and pulse until combined. (It's important to use boiling water rather than just hot or warm water because the extra heat activates the flavors.)
3. Serve immediately with tortilla chips or store, covered, in the refrigerator up to a week.

TARA'S TIP

One regular or large bunch of cilantro is roughly 2 cups coarsely chopped leaves and tender stems. Adjust this amount to suit your taste. I like to use about 1½ cups chopped.

There isn't a perfect substitute for El Pato spicy tomato sauce, but if you can't find it, use a small can of traditional tomato sauce with a few splashes of hot sauce and increase the garlic powder to 1 teaspoon.

MAKES

1¾ CUPS
CHUTNEY, ABOUT
28 CROSTINI

HANDS-ON TIME

25 MINUTES

TOTAL TIME

50 MINUTES

mandarin and prosciutto crostini

THIS IS MY ESSENTIAL APPETIZER: toasted crostini topped with a little slice of salty prosciutto and some tangy mandarin and shallot chutney. I've been known to make a full meal of these little bites.

Double the caramelized shallot and mandarin portion of this recipe and keep the extra in the fridge. It works beautifully on top of chicken or a roast ham sandwich—or even for your next batch of crostini bites.

2 cups sliced shallots, sliced root to tip

½ teaspoon kosher salt

1 tablespoon olive oil

½ cup white balsamic vinegar

½ cup light brown sugar

1 bay leaf

1 teaspoon crushed coriander seeds

1 cup fresh mandarin or clementine segments, roughly chopped

1 recipe Crostini (below), prepared

14 slices prosciutto

Toasted hazelnuts, crushed

Fresh thyme

1. In a medium, nonstick skillet over medium-low heat, sauté the shallots and salt in olive oil, stirring often, until soft and translucent, 10 to 12 minutes. Add the vinegar, brown sugar, bay leaf, and coriander seeds and let simmer until vinegar is reduced and almost gone, 10 to 12 minutes more. Stir in the mandarin segments. Remove from heat and let cool slightly.

2. Top crostini with a half piece of prosciutto and a spoonful of the mandarin chutney. Sprinkle with hazelnuts and thyme leaves.

LOOKS DELICIOUS Whenever I caramelize onions or shallots, I slice them from their root to the tip. Slicing them crosswise into rings or half-moons causes them to cook into long, stringy worms. The root-to-tip method allows the shallot or onion to hold its shape, looks better, and is easier to eat.

TARA'S TIP

The caramelized shallot mixture can be prepared ahead of time and stored in an airtight container in the refrigerator. When you are ready to make your nibbles, gently heat the shallot mixture in a nonstick pan and then stir in the chopped mandarin segments.

CROSTINI

AN OLIVE-OIL-TOASTED baguette is a staple for all sorts of snack and appetizer creations. This one is so simple, you won't need a recipe after making them once.

1 baguette, sliced ¼-inch thick

¼ cup olive oil

Kosher salt

1. Heat oven to 375°F. Brush slices of bread lightly with olive oil on both sides. Lay slices flat on rimmed baking sheets and sprinkle with some salt.

2. Bake, rotating pans halfway through, until lightly golden and crisp, 10 to 12 minutes. Let cool.

3. Store crostinis in a zip-top bag for up to 3 days.

mile-high buttermilk biscuits

THESE BISCUITS are the quintessential lofty quick bread that serves as a delectable vehicle for butter and jam, but can be transformed into a fantastic side for BBQ, fried chicken, or sausage gravy.

I make these biscuits extra-large and extra tall so they hold up to the chicken and slaw in my Chicken and Biscuits with Honey Butter (page 99). Make them smaller if you're serving them for breakfast or a side. The secret is to not overwork the dough, and just pat it into shape rather than roll it with a rolling pin.

MAKES

8 LARGE BISCUITS

HANDS-ON TIME

10 MINUTES

TOTAL TIME

30 MINUTES

4 cups all-purpose flour, plus more for dusting

4 teaspoons baking powder

1 teaspoon baking soda

1½ teaspoons salt

1 teaspoon granulated sugar

1 cup unsalted butter, cut into ½-inch pieces

2 cups buttermilk

1. Heat oven to 375°F. In a medium bowl, whisk together flour, baking powder, baking soda, salt, and sugar.
2. Using a pastry blender, cut butter pieces into flour mixture until it resembles coarse crumbs.
3. Add the buttermilk and stir with a rubber spatula just until mixture comes together; dough will be sticky.
4. Transfer dough to a lightly floured work surface; use floured fingers to pat dough into a 1½-inch thick rectangle. Use a floured 3- to 3¼-inch round biscuit cutter or cookie cutter to cut biscuits as closely together as possible to minimize scraps. Use an up-and-down motion to cut biscuits rather than a side-to-side twist. (I like to gently bundle any scraps together and bake alongside the biscuits for a little snack.)
5. Transfer biscuits to a baking sheet and bake until lightly browned, 18 to 20 minutes. Remove from oven and cool on a wire rack.

TARA'S TIP

Shortcut your efforts and make rustic-looking biscuits. Forego the biscuit cutter and cut formed dough into rectangles or squares with a chef's knife. Square biscuits taste just as good as round ones!

BITES, DIPS, AND SNACKS

double-cheese garlic bread

MAKES

8 TO 10 SERVINGS,
1 LOAF

HANDS-ON TIME

20 MINUTES

TOTAL TIME

30 MINUTES

THIS GARLIC BREAD is the perfect side to spaghetti, my Sublime Sausage Pesto Lasagna (page 159), or your favorite soup or salad. Serve slices of this cheesy, flavorful bread alongside a bowl of simple marinara for a fun party snack. It's delicious however you share it.

1 loaf French bread

½ cup (1 stick) unsalted butter, softened

⅔ cup grated Parmesan

⅔ cup grated mozzarella

2 cloves garlic, minced

1 teaspoon kosher salt

2 tablespoons chopped flat-leaf parsley, or 1 tablespoon dried parsley flakes

1. Heat oven to 350°F. Line a baking sheet with parchment or foil.
2. Cut loaf of bread in half lengthwise to create two long, flat pieces.
3. In a medium mixing bowl, beat together butter, Parmesan, mozzarella, garlic, salt, and parsley with an electric mixer until well combined.
4. Spread half of the mixture on the cut side of each half of the bread and place, butter-side-up, on prepared baking sheet.
5. Bake until bread is heated through, 7 to 8 minutes. Switch oven to the broiler setting and broil on high until cheese top is turning golden and melted, 1 to 2 minutes more.
6. Cut bread into pieces and serve immediately.

TARA'S TIP

My favorite thing about this straightforward recipe is that I can make batches of the flavorful, cheese-garlic-butter ahead of time and keep it in the freezer. Follow the directions in step 3 and transfer butter to freezer bags or containers. (Or roll it in parchment.) Label and freeze each container for up to 3 months. Pull one out and thaw when you want garlic bread with half the effort.

LOOKS DELICIOUS If you have extra parsley on hand, sprinkle baked bread with fresh parsley right before serving. This brightens the look and gives a little extra herb flavor.

SALADS, BOWLS, AND DRESSINGS

salmon, veggie, and carrot-ginger rice bowl

MAKES

4 SERVINGS

HANDS-ON TIME

25 MINUTES

TOTAL TIME

50 MINUTES

SKIP THE TAKE-OUT rice bowl from your local lunch haunt and make your own at home. This dish is a light, yet filling, flavorful meal. I used my so-good-you-could-drink-it Tara's Carrot-Ginger Dressing as the saucy drizzle, leaving the salty sweet teriyaki glaze for the baked salmon.

Zucchini noodles, crunchy cucumbers, and creamy avocado compete as the shining stars next to the quick-cooking salmon. In the time it takes the rice to cook, your meal is already prepped and ready to go.

1½ cups short-grain sushi rice

3 tablespoons low-sodium soy sauce

3 tablespoons light brown sugar

¼ teaspoon garlic powder

½ teaspoon sesame oil

1 (16-ounce) salmon filet, cut into 4 pieces

2 medium zucchini, spiralized

2 Persian cucumbers, halved and thinly sliced

1 medium ripe avocado, pitted and sliced

1 recipe Tara's Carrot-Ginger Dressing (page 50), prepared

Chopped cilantro

Toasted sesame seeds

> **TARA'S TIP**
> For a quick shortcut, use store-bought teriyaki sauce in place of my soy sauce mixture.

1. Rinse and cook rice according to package directions. When done, set aside and keep warm.
2. Heat broiler to high and place rack 4 to 6 inches from the element. Line a baking sheet or broiler pan with foil.
3. While rice cooks, in a small bowl, mix together the soy sauce, brown sugar, garlic powder, and sesame oil until the sugar is dissolved.
4. Dip the salmon pieces in the soy sauce mixture and place on prepared pan. Broil 2 minutes, and then brush with more sauce. Rotate pan and broil 2 minutes more. Repeat brushing, and then rotate pan again, and broil a final 1 to 2 minutes, until salmon is cooked to medium (145°F on an instant-read thermometer). Remove and set aside.
5. Assemble bowls by dividing rice among four bowls; top with zucchini noodles, cucumber, and avocado. Break salmon into pieces and add, then drizzle with Tara's Carrot-Ginger Dressing and top with cilantro and sesame seeds.

LOOKS DELICIOUS I use a handheld vegetable spiralizer for my zucchini, but you don't have to have a special tool to enjoy this recipe. You can thinly slice the zucchini or even dice it and toss with the cucumbers to make your own veggie mixture.

MAKES

⅔ CUP

HANDS-ON TIME

12 MINUTES

TOTAL TIME

12 MINUTES

tara's carrot-ginger dressing

THIS DRESSING achieves the perfect balance of tang, sweet, seasoning, and umami. The ponzu and soy sauce bring the umami, and are every bit as important as the other ingredients. The carrots, onion, and ginger all play a role in making this taste just like the authentic dressing at your favorite Japanese restaurant.

The dressing is great with salad or rice and noodle bowls. Keep a jar on hand in the fridge; it stores well up to 2 weeks. I promise you'll beg to eat your veggies if this dressing is involved.

TARA'S TIP

Ponzu is a tart, thin, dark-brown liquid infused with rice wine, vinegar, fish flakes, seaweed, and yuzu, a Japanese citrus. You can find it in the Asian section of your grocery store. I recommend taking the time to seek it out. If you can't find it, however, use a mixture of lime juice and rice wine vinegar with a dash of fish sauce in its place.

3½ tablespoons peeled, chopped fresh ginger

4 carrots, peeled and cut into pieces (1½ cups)

½ small yellow onion, roughly chopped

⅔ cup rice vinegar

2 tablespoons ponzu

1 teaspoon sesame oil

2 tablespoons low-sodium soy sauce

1 tablespoon granulated sugar

¼ cup water

⅓ cup canola or avocado oil

1. In a powerful blender, combine all ingredients except the oil. Blend until very smooth.
2. Whisk in the oil or pulse in blender for just 2 seconds. Mixing the oil too much will change the color and texture of the dressing. Serve immediately or store in an airtight container in the refrigerator up to 2 weeks.

watermelon arugula salad

MAKES

4 TO 6 SERVINGS,
8 CUPS SALAD

HANDS-ON TIME

15 MINUTES

TOTAL TIME

15 MINUTES

THE PEPPERY BITE of arugula paired with sweet, juicy watermelon and tangy tomatoes makes for a fabulous combination. The pine nuts add a rich, buttery-soft, nutty complement to the bright and vibrant salad.

Pair this with any vinaigrette, but it's especially tasty with Raspberry Balsamic Vinaigrette. The fruity flavors mingle so well together.

5 cups (5 ounces) baby arugula	⅓ cup pine nuts, toasted
4 cups cubed watermelon	1 recipe Raspberry Balsamic Vinaigrette (below), prepared
1 cup yellow cherry tomatoes, cut in half	

1. In a large bowl, gently toss together the arugula, watermelon, and cherry tomatoes.
2. Top with pine nuts and serve with Raspberry Balsamic Vinaigrette.

LOOKS DELICIOUS The colors of this salad are so appealing. There is such a fun variety of produce, I encourage you to play around with different colors! Try yellow watermelon and red or orange tomatoes to keep it bright and vibrant.

TARA'S TIP

Cut the watermelon into cubes smaller than 1 inch so they are easy to eat in a single bite. For a variation on the look, add thin slices of melon and let them break up as you toss the salad.

raspberry balsamic vinaigrette

MAKES

1 CUP

HANDS-ON TIME

8 MINUTES

TOTAL TIME

8 MINUTES

I ADD HONEY or a spoonful of sugar to my vinegar in dressings to add depth of flavor and cut the piquant acid. Raspberry preserves are a great swap for a sweetener and create a vinaigrette with a surprising note.

Balsamic vinegar also pairs well with rich berry flavors, so feel free to swap raspberry for current, blackberry, or even strawberry jams, depending on what you have on hand.

⅓ cup balsamic vinegar	½ teaspoon ground black pepper
2 tablespoons water	1 tablespoon finely chopped shallot
4 teaspoons raspberry preserves	⅔ cup extra-virgin olive oil
¼ teaspoon kosher salt	

1. In a medium bowl, stir together all ingredients except the oil until well combined.
2. Slowly add the oil, whisking constantly. Serve or store in a covered container at room temperature up to 3 days or in the refrigerator up to 3 weeks. If chilled, bring to room temperature and shake well before serving.

kale and cabbage slaw with radishes and pepitas

MAKES

4 TO 6 SERVINGS,
ABOUT 6 CUPS
SALAD

HANDS-ON TIME

10 MINUTES

TOTAL TIME

20 MINUTES

THIS SLAW reminds me of kale's trendy goodness every time I make it. I slice the kale thinly, then let it marinate in dressing for a few minutes. The vinegar softens the hearty, cruciferous leaves and makes them tender, yet still crunchy. These techniques create the perfect bite and a flavorful salad I'll happily call delicious.

This kale slaw can hold its own out of the bowl, but it's also great as a slaw for tacos, awesome with black beans and grilled chicken, and downright delicious on a steak salad.

3 cups finely sliced and chopped kale, thick stems removed	½ cup thinly sliced radishes
1½ cups thinly sliced cabbage	½ cup roasted pepitas
1 cup julienned or shredded carrots	1 recipe Subtly Spicy Cilantro-Lime Dressing (below), prepared

1. In a large bowl, toss together the kale, cabbage, carrots, radishes, and pepitas.
2. Drizzle with several tablespoons Subtly Spicy Cilantro-Lime Dressing and toss. Let salad sit for 10 minutes and then toss with more dressing and serve.

subtly spicy cilantro-lime dressing

MAKES

1 CUP

HANDS-ON TIME

8 MINUTES

TOTAL TIME

8 MINUTES

THIS DRESSING may be the sole reason limes exist. It is so luscious, and the spice is perfectly balanced. No salad is safe when this dressing is on hand! I drizzle it on anything relatively green served in a bowl and even use it for a marinade for chicken or skirt steak.

¼ cup fresh lime juice	¼ teaspoon kosher salt
2 tablespoons apple cider vinegar	1 tablespoon honey
¼ teaspoon cayenne pepper	2 tablespoons chopped cilantro
½ teaspoon ground cumin	⅔ cup canola or avocado oil

1. In a medium bowl, stir together all of the ingredients except the oil until well combined.
2. Slowly add the oil, whisking constantly. Serve or store in a covered container at room temperature up to 3 days or in the refrigerator up to 3 weeks. If chilled, bring to room temperature and shake well before serving.

magic chopped salad

MAKES

6 SERVINGS, ABOUT
9 CUPS SALAD

HANDS-ON TIME

20 MINUTES

TOTAL TIME

20 MINUTES

MY FRIEND SUSAN dubbed this "Magic Salad," and, I must admit, the combination of crunchy greens and vegetables paired with a divine dressing (like the Pickled Red Onion and Herb Vinaigrette) make it truly sublime. The herbs in the dressing are key, as is the tangy and lightly sweetened sherry vinegar that quick-pickles the onions.

The complex, flavorful salad is great for a crowd and can be served with a big dinner or turned into a weeknight meal by adding grilled chicken or roasted salmon.

1 head romaine, chopped (4 cups)

3 cups baby arugula, chopped

1 cup chopped haricot verts or thin green beans

1 cup Persian cucumber, halved and sliced into half-moons

1 cup snow peas, cut into halves or thirds on the bias

¼ head purple cabbage, thinly sliced and chopped

½ cup toasted hazelnuts, coarsely chopped

1 cup shredded Gouda cheese

1 Recipe Pickled Red Onion and Herb Vinaigrette (below), prepared

1. In a large bowl, toss together chopped greens, haricot verts, cucumbers, snow peas, and cabbage.
2. Just before serving, toss with hazelnuts, cheese, and dressing.

pickled red onion and herb vinaigrette

MAKES

1½ CUPS

HANDS-ON TIME

20 MINUTES

TOTAL TIME

20 MINUTES

DELICIOUS on lots of salads, this dressing is particularly tasty on the Magic Chopped Salad. The choice of herbs is up to you, but I suggest a heavier hand on the basil and parsley with just a bit of oregano and thyme. That said, all the herbs listed create a depth of flavor that is obvious but not overpowering.

½ cup sherry vinegar

½ teaspoon kosher salt

2 tablespoons sugar or honey

⅓ cup finely chopped fresh herbs (any mix of basil, oregano, thyme, marjoram, or parsley)

½ cup extra-virgin olive oil

½ cup thinly sliced red onion, coarsely chopped

1. In a medium bowl, whisk together vinegar, salt, sugar, and herbs. Slowly add the oil, whisking constantly.
2. Stir in the onion and let dressing sit for at least 10 minutes before serving.
3. Store dressing in a covered container at room temperature up to a day or in the refrigerator up to 1 week. Shake well or stir before using.

TARA'S TIP It's worth making a double batch so you can keep this dressing around a few days. It's glorious on any bowl of greens or on steamed, roasted, or grilled veggies.

butter lettuce, fig, and ricotta salata salad

MAKES

4 TO 6 SERVINGS

HANDS-ON TIME

15 MINUTES

TOTAL TIME

15 MINUTES

A SIMPLE, yet sophisticated salad. The soft and delicate Bibb lettuce works beautifully with ultra-sweet figs and slightly salty Ricotta Salata, a pungent Italian sheep's milk that can be sliced. Adding a robust vinaigrette like the Pistachio Dill Vinaigrette complements the softer, buttery lettuce layers.

1 head Butter or Bibb lettuce

1½ cups fresh figs, cut into halves or quarters

2 ounces Ricotta Salata, thinly sliced (about ½ cup)

1 recipe Pistachio Dill Vinaigrette (below), prepared

Roasted pistachios, for garnish

Chopped dill, for garnish

1. Tear very large lettuce leaves in half; leave small ones whole. Arrange on a platter or in a bowl and top with figs.
2. Use a vegetable peeler to shave the Ricotta Salata over the top.
3. Drizzle with Pistachio Dill Vinaigrette and garnish with pistachios and dill.

LOOKS DELICIOUS This makes a pretty presentation on a platter. Tear large lettuce leaves in half and use smaller leaves as overlapping cups to hold the other tasty ingredients.

pistachio dill vinaigrette

MAKES

1¼ CUPS

HANDS-ON TIME

15 MINUTES

TOTAL TIME

15 MINUTES

THIS VINAIGRETTE is so hearty and delicious, nutty and crunchy, tangy and sweet, it's practically a meal itself! But alas, it's truly a dressing and completely delicious on greens and veggies. Still, grab a fork and dig in!

½ cup white balsamic vinegar

½ teaspoon kosher salt

3 tablespoons honey

¼ cup finely chopped roasted pistachios

¼ cup finely chopped scallions

1 tablespoon finely chopped dill

½ cup extra-virgin olive oil

1. In a medium bowl, whisk together the vinegar, salt, honey and pistachios.
2. Add the scallions and dill and whisk together while slowly drizzling in the olive oil.
3. Store dressing in a covered container at room temperature up to 1 day or in the refrigerator up to 3 days.

sesame ginger dressing

MAKES

1 CUP

HANDS-ON TIME

8 MINUTES

TOTAL TIME

8 MINUTES

THIS IS A STAPLE dressing at my house, and any leftover cabbage, hearty greens, or grated carrots get turned into a slaw and topped with it. Blanched green beans, sautéed snow peas, and steamed bok choy succumb to a drizzle as well. Add grilled chicken or sliced steak to a salad along with this dressing and slices of citrus, either oranges or clementines, and enjoy.

¼ cup rice wine vinegar	1 teaspoon freshly grated ginger
¼ cup fresh lime juice	½ teaspoon sesame oil
½ tablespoon low-sodium soy sauce	2 teaspoons toasted sesame seeds
2 tablespoons honey or light brown sugar	⅔ cup canola or avocado oil

1. In a medium bowl, stir together all ingredients except the oil until well combined.
2. Slowly add the oil, whisking constantly. Store dressing in a covered container at room temperature up to 3 days or in the refrigerator up to 2 weeks. Shake or stir before using, as dressing can separate.

tangy tomato vinaigrette

MAKES

1 CUP

HANDS-ON TIME

8 MINUTES

TOTAL TIME

8 MINUTES

THIS IS LIKE your grandma's marinara, or as my Italian-American neighbors in New Jersey call it, "gravy" for your salad! Lighter, and more tangy and fitting than marinara for a salad, it retains that savory tomato-and-herb flavor. This quick vinaigrette is easy to make, and it keeps well in the fridge, which makes it perfect for those clean-out-the-produce-drawer salads.

⅓ cup tomato juice	2 tablespoons finely chopped shallot
3 tablespoons red wine vinegar	½ tablespoon light brown sugar
½ teaspoon kosher salt	1 teaspoon dried oregano
½ teaspoon ground black pepper	⅔ cup extra-virgin olive oil

1. In a medium bowl, whisk together all ingredients except the oil.
2. Slowly add the oil, whisking constantly. Store dressing in a covered container at room temperature up to 3 days or in the refrigerator up to 2 weeks. If chilled, bring to room temperature and shake well before serving.

lemon parmesan vinaigrette

MAKES

1 CUP

HANDS-ON TIME

6 MINUTES

TOTAL TIME

6 MINUTES

LEMON AND PARMESAN are a combination made in umami heaven. Parmesan that has aged 24 to 36 months develops flavorful qualities as amino acids break down creating glutamic acid (the umami acid). Lemon, another flavor powerhouse, is like salt and highlights the flavors of other ingredients—sort of like a validating friend who brings out the best in you! Put these two happy things together and you get a dressing that brings out the best in your greens.

¼ cup fresh lemon juice

2 tablespoons white wine vinegar

¼ teaspoon kosher salt

¼ teaspoon ground black pepper

1 tablespoon granulated sugar

3 tablespoons finely grated Parmesan

½ cup extra-virgin olive oil

1. In a medium bowl, whisk together all ingredients except the oil until the sugar is dissolved.
2. Slowly pour in the oil, whisking constantly. Store dressing in a covered container at room temperature up to 2 days or in the refrigerator up to 2 weeks. If chilled, bring to room temperature and shake well before serving.

classic french dijon vinaigrette

ALL HAIL THE KING of dressings! I imagine Louis the XIV eating this on his greens and lardons at the Palace of Versailles. Needless to say, it's quite classic and very French.

Traditionally, a French Dijon dressing relies on tarragon to create a unique flavor. Fresh herbs are a must here, so if you can't find fresh tarragon—or don't care for its mild licorice flavor—don't use the dry stuff. Use 1 teaspoon of fresh thyme instead.

It's great with red leaf, arugula, frisée, or endive and some walnuts and goat cheese, too.

⅓ cup white wine vinegar

½ teaspoon kosher salt

½ teaspoon ground black pepper

1 tablespoon Dijon mustard

1 teaspoon granulated sugar

2 teaspoons chopped tarragon

½ cup extra-virgin olive oil

1. In a medium bowl, whisk together all ingredients except the oil.
2. Slowly add the oil, whisking constantly. Store dressing in a covered container at room temperature up to 1 day or in the refrigerator up to 2 weeks. If chilled, bring to room temperature and shake well before serving.

MAKES

1 CUP

HANDS-ON TIME

8 MINUTES

TOTAL TIME

8 MINUTES

TARA'S TIP

A seasoned cook's tip is to use your nearly empty jar of Dijon mustard as the container for your next batch of dressing in order to take advantage of the last morsels of mustard. This recipe is a little large for a mustard jar, so I'd suggest shaking everything but the oil in the jar, then whisking in the oil in a bowl.

MAKES

4 TO 6 SERVINGS

HANDS-ON TIME

15 MINUTES

TOTAL TIME

15 MINUTES

white bean salad with italian tuna

THIS CAN BE so much more than a salad! Use it as a topper for crostini to create a delicious app, as a side for snack boards, on pasta, or add it to a big bowl of salad greens. Of course, it is so good on its own, it can be a complete lunch.

Canned tuna is one of those ingredients most folks don't want to admit they eat. Or perhaps you feel it's meant only for "that" sandwich—you know the one. Forget your preconceived notions; I've given it a chic treatment, and made over a very classic Italian dish. Don't be surprised if the resulting salad, mixed with bright citrus, strong radicchio, and creamy beans becomes a new favorite.

TARA'S TIP
New York City markets often stock Italian tuna packed in the most luxurious olive oil; it really is divine. Albacore tuna packed in oil from the can is a close second. Just don't get tuna packed in water. The oil gives the tuna a silky and rich quality and flavor, and a bit of sophistication.

1 (14.5-ounce) can white cannellini beans, drained and rinsed

2 tablespoons finely minced shallot

1 cup radicchio, torn

1 (5-ounce) jar or can Italian tuna, packed in olive oil, drained

Zest of 1 lemon

2 tablespoons fresh lemon juice

2 tablespoons red wine vinegar

½ teaspoon kosher salt

½ teaspoon ground black pepper

2 tablespoons extra-virgin olive oil

2 cups watercress

¼ cup shaved Parmesan

1. In a large bowl, toss together the beans, shallot, and radicchio. Gently break tuna into large pieces and add to the beans.

2. In another bowl, whisk together lemon zest, lemon juice, vinegar, salt, pepper, and olive oil. Drizzle over tuna and beans.

3. Garnish with watercress and Parmesan and serve.

LOOKS DELICIOUS The mix of red radicchio and green watercress really makes this salad pretty. There are a lot of other colorful greens you can swap in to get the same effect. Try arugula or baby spinach in place of the watercress, or red endive or cabbage in place of the radicchio if you'd like.

dill and feta orzo salad

THIS IS ONE of my favorite pasta salads. It's so easy to put together and packs up perfectly for picnics, shines at a BBQ, or makes for a lovely lunch with some shrimp and arugula. The fresh dill is the unsung hero, making the everyday veggies and pasta pop. Dill is sometimes scarce at a typical grocery, so if you're not finding it but craving this salad, a handful of chopped parsley or basil can fill in.

1 cup uncooked orzo

1 teaspoon lemon zest

2 tablespoons extra-virgin olive oil, divided

2 tablespoons fresh lemon juice

¼ red onion, thinly sliced and chopped

2 Persian cucumbers, cut into ½-inch pieces

1 cup cherry tomatoes, quartered

3 tablespoons chopped dill, plus more for garnish

½ cup feta, crumbled, plus more for garnish

Ground black pepper

1. Cook orzo in very salty water according to package directions; don't overcook. Drain and transfer to a large bowl. While still warm, toss with lemon zest, lemon juice, and 1 tablespoon olive oil. Set aside to cool, stirring occasionally so it doesn't clump.

2. When orzo is cool, add red onion, cucumbers, cherry tomatoes, and dill, and toss to combine. Stir in the feta and remaining 1 tablespoon olive oil.

3. Serve with extra feta, dill, and black pepper.

MAKES

4 TO 6 SERVINGS, ABOUT 6 CUPS SALAD

HANDS-ON TIME

10 MINUTES

TOTAL TIME

35 MINUTES

TARA'S TIP

The Pistachio Dill Vinaigrette (page 57) is delicious on this pasta salad. If you have the vinaigrette on hand, skip the lemon juice and olive oil and add 2 tablespoons of the vinaigrette to the pasta after cooking and 2 more tablespoons when you add the feta.

SALADS, BOWLS, AND DRESSINGS

SIDE LOVE

roasted cauliflower and smoky romesco

MAKES

4 TO 6 SERVINGS

HANDS-ON TIME

15 MINUTES

TOTAL TIME

40 MINUTES

THIS IS A SIDE DISH I threw together from bits and bobs in the fridge; it turned out amazing! I love roasted veggies, especially cauliflower. Pairing it with my romesco and a kick of smoky paprika is gold—pure gold.

Romesco is a sauce made from a lovely mixture of roasted red peppers, almonds, and other good things. I swapped the sweet paprika in my Savory Romesco and Almond Tart with smoked paprika for this dreamy roasted veggie condiment.

1 head cauliflower, trimmed, large florets cut into thick slices	1 recipe Romesco Sauce (page 153), prepared with smoked paprika
3 tablespoons olive oil	⅓ cup crushed, roasted, and salted almonds
1 teaspoon kosher salt	2 tablespoons chopped flat-leaf parsley
Pinch ground black pepper	

1. Heat oven to 425°F. Toss cauliflower florets with olive oil, salt, and pepper. Roast on a rimmed baking sheet until just tender and deep golden brown in parts, 15 to 20 minutes.

2. Spoon some of the romesco sauce on a platter and top with the roasted cauliflower. Top with the crushed almonds, parsley, and extra pepper.

3. Reserve remaining romesco for another meal. It will keep in the fridge for up to a week.

LOOKS DELICIOUS The parsley is both a garnish and an addition of fresh, herby flavor in this dish. You can certainly enjoy it without the parsley, but the green does wonders for both that burst of freshness and the eye appeal.

MAKES

10 TO 12 SERVINGS

HANDS-ON TIME

30 MINUTES

TOTAL TIME

1 HOUR 15 MINUTES

caramelized onion and smoked gouda mac and cheese

THIS COMFORT FOOD perfection will be the most popular dish on the table. I'm stating facts here, people! Who doesn't love mac and cheese, and when it's mixed with caramelized onions—those melty, savory-sweet gems—I defy you to resist. The smoked cheese is borderline overkill, but it pairs perfectly with the sweet onions in the creamy béchamel sauce pooled inside the shell pasta. Sure you can share this as a side dish, but I won't tell if you decide to keep it to yourself.

TARA'S TIP

Shell pasta is heavenly for this mac and cheese. The little pasta cups hold just the right amount of cheesy, caramelized-onion goodness. Can you use a different shaped pasta? Of course! Don't let the pasta shape hold you back from making this!

1 medium yellow onion, finely diced

4 tablespoons olive oil, divided

¼ cup water

1 (16-ounce) box medium shell pasta

6 tablespoons unsalted butter

6 tablespoons all-purpose flour

4 cups whole milk, warmed

2½ teaspoons kosher salt

⅛ teaspoon cayenne pepper

¼ teaspoon ground black pepper

7 ounces smoked Gouda cheese, shredded (3 cups)

11 ounces Monterey Jack cheese, shredded (4 cups)

1 cup Panko breadcrumbs

1 teaspoon chopped thyme

1. Heat 1 tablespoon olive oil in a medium nonstick skillet over medium-high heat. Add onions and sauté 1 minute. Add water and cover pan with a lid. Cook 5 minutes. Remove lid, reduce heat to medium, and cook onions, stirring frequently, until caramelized and dark golden brown, about 15 minutes. Set aside.

2. Heat oven to 400°F. Cook pasta in very salty water according to package directions. Drain and set aside.

3. In the pasta pot or a large saucepan, over medium heat, melt butter. Whisk in the flour and stir until the mixture is light brown and smells nutty, about 3 minutes. Slowly add the warm milk, whisking constantly. When all the milk has been added, bring to a simmer before stirring in salt, cayenne pepper, black pepper, and shredded cheeses. Reduce heat to low and cook, stirring, until the sauce has thickened and cheese is melted, 3 to 5 minutes.

4. In a small bowl, combine the breadcrumbs, thyme, and remaining 3 tablespoons olive oil.

5. Add caramelized onion and cooked pasta to the cheese sauce and toss to coat. Pour into a 9-by-13-inch pan or 3-quart casserole dish. Top with breadcrumb mixture and bake until top has turned golden brown and the cheese sauce is bubbling, 40 to 45 minutes. Let cool 10 minutes before serving.

garlic and sumac roasted broccoli with sweet dates

ONE OF THE MOST perfect veggies for roasting is broccoli. It takes on an entirely different flavor—earthy and charred but still sweet. So often broccoli is paired with cheese, but
I like to keep it simple and let this vegetable shine.

Roasting it with sliced garlic is aromatic, but not overpowering. Adding a few sweet
dates elevates it to an entertaining-worthy side dish.

MAKES

4 TO 6 SERVINGS

HANDS-ON TIME

10 MINUTES

TOTAL TIME

20 MINUTES

2 pounds broccoli	¾ teaspoon kosher salt
3 tablespoons olive oil	½ teaspoon ground black pepper
2 cloves garlic, thinly sliced	4 to 5 dates, sliced crosswise on the bias
1 teaspoon sumac	

TARA'S TIP

Sumac is a spice native to the Middle East and has a tangy, citrusy, almost-lemon flavor. If you don't have any on hand, substitute with 1 teaspoon lemon zest.

1. Heat oven to 450°F. Place a rimmed baking sheet in the oven to heat while you prepare the broccoli.

2. Cut broccoli into small florets, slicing large florets in half. (You'll need 6 to 7 cups of florets.) In a large bowl, toss broccoli with olive oil, garlic, sumac, salt, and pepper.

3. Carefully remove the hot pan from the oven and transfer the broccoli mixture to the baking sheet, using a rubber scraper to get all the good bits out of the bowl.

4. Return pan to the oven and roast broccoli until tender and a bit charred, about 15 minutes.

5. Add dates and serve broccoli immediately.

SIDE LOVE

LOOKS DELICIOUS I heat the pan before roasting the broccoli so the vegetable can immediately begin to sear and cook. This creates tender broccoli that isn't soggy or wilted.

cheese-and-herb potato gratin

ROUNDS OF ALTERNATING sweet and white potatoes tossed with herbs and spices are baked up with cheese in a gratin that is as delicious as it is impressive. It's worthy of any holiday table yet simple enough for a regular day.

Choose your preference when it comes to the cheese, but Gruyère will add a sweet, nutty flavor to the gratin while a sharp white cheddar like Tillamook is creamy and complex and adds an aged, bold flavor to the potatoes and herbs.

Allow me to sing the praises of a spice cupboard. I'll wager you have a collection of dried herbs and seasonings in the pantry just waiting to be used. Use them! This will let you focus your prep time on slicing those potatoes. (Tip: get a mandolin!)

MAKES

8 TO 10 SERVINGS

HANDS-ON TIME

20 MINUTES

TOTAL TIME

1 HOUR 20 MINUTES

3 medium sweet potatoes

6 small Yukon gold potatoes

1 teaspoon kosher salt

¼ teaspoon ground black pepper

¾ teaspoon garlic powder

1½ teaspoons dried parsley

½ teaspoon dried thyme

½ teaspoon ground sage

½ teaspoon dried rosemary

8 ounces Gruyère or sharp white cheddar, grated (2 cups)

½ cup thinly sliced yellow onion, chopped

½ cup whole milk or half-and-half

½ cup low-sodium chicken broth

> ### TARA'S TIP
> This recipe is a great way to use the fresh herbs you have left over from a holiday meal or the last bits after a week of cooking. I use fresh herbs in the spring and summer when they are plentiful and cheap. I'll use my spice cupboard in the winter months. Use double the amount of fresh as you would dry.

1. Preheat oven to 375°F. Peel potatoes, and, using a mandolin or vegetable slicer, cut into very thin slices. In a large bowl, gently toss potatoes with salt, pepper, garlic powder, parsley, thyme, sage, rosemary, cheese, and onion, until everything is evenly mixed. Be careful not to break the thin potato slices.

2. Working with a small handful of potatoes at a time, gently line up coated slices in a 10-inch cast-iron skillet or 2-quart baking dish. Pour milk and broth over potatoes. Cover pan with foil and seal around edges.

3. Bake 50 minutes and remove foil. Continue to bake until potatoes are tender and top is golden, 15 to 20 minutes more. You can test the potatoes with a knife to see if they are tender throughout. Cool slightly and serve hot.

LOOKS DELICIOUS You can layer the cheese and potato slices flat in a baking dish as a classic gratin, but this presentation is all about the wow! Standing up the slices, whether in rows or a circle, creates an impressive look and is worth the extra minutes to arrange them before cooking.

MAKES

6 TO 8 SERVINGS

HANDS-ON TIME

15 MINUTES

TOTAL TIME

50 MINUTES

glazed, bacon-wrapped sweet potatoes

IF YOU'RE ASKED to bring a side dish to Thanksgiving dinner, you're cooking Sunday dinner, or you're simply making a weeknight meal, my vote is to include this side dish. Melt-in-your mouth sweet potatoes, a savory-sweet glaze, and crisped bacon hardly have to campaign. They are a shoo-in for winning over any party involved.

4 medium (2½ pounds) sweet potatoes, peeled

1½ tablespoons olive oil

¾ teaspoon kosher salt

¼ teaspoon ground black pepper

12 slices bacon

1 recipe Savory-Sweet Apricot Glaze (page 172), prepared with thyme

Thyme for garnish

1. Heat oven to 400°F. Line a rimmed baking sheet with foil.
2. Slice potatoes lengthwise in ¾-inch thick slices. You should get about 3 slices from each potato.
3. In a medium bowl, toss potatoes with olive oil, salt, and pepper.
4. Wrap a slice of bacon around the middle of each potato slice, gently stretching if needed, and overlapping a bit on the ends. Place slices with the ends of the bacon down so the potato holds it in place on the baking sheet. For smaller potato slices, you can use a smaller piece of bacon.
5. Bake 15 minutes, then gently turn potatoes over and bake until potatoes are tender and bacon is getting crisped, 10 to 15 minutes more.
6. Brush potatoes with Savory-Sweet Apricot Glaze and bake another 5 to 8 minutes, or until bacon reaches desired crispness.
7. Remove from oven, brush with additional glaze, and sprinkle with extra thyme to serve.

TARA'S TIP

Depending on its thickness, the bacon may curl up as it cooks instead of hugging the slice of sweet potato. Have a few toothpicks on hand and use them to hold the bacon in place while it bakes. Remove them for serving, of course.

lemon-herb veggie couscous with raisins and almonds

MAKES

6 TO 8 SERVINGS,
7 CUPS COUSCOUS

HANDS-ON TIME

35 MINUTES

TOTAL TIME

1 HOUR 5 MINUTES

TRADITIONAL COUSCOUS dishes often have nuts and dried fruit nestled between the pillowy pasta grains. I keep those flavors and swap in Israeli couscous, often called pearl couscous; the little pearls are fantastic with the golden raisins and almonds, but even better with the lemony veggies. Toast the couscous pearls in a dry pan before boiling for an extra nutty flavor.

1½ cups dry Israeli or pearl couscous

1 recipe Lemon and Parmesan Vegetable Medley (page 79), prepared

2 tablespoons chopped basil

1 teaspoon chopped thyme

½ cup sliced almonds, toasted

½ cup golden raisins

1. Heat a medium pot over medium-high heat and add couscous. Heat couscous in the dry pan to toast, stirring frequently, 1 to 3 minutes. The pearls will turn golden brown and smell nutty. Remove the pearls to a bowl.

2. Fill pot halfway with water, generously salt, and bring to a boil. Add the toasted couscous, reduce heat, and simmer until couscous is just done, 6 to 8 minutes. It will still be a bit toothsome. Don't overcook it or it will be mush. Immediately drain in a mesh colander and transfer to a bowl.

3. Toss with prepared Lemon and Parmesan Vegetable Medley. Add basil, thyme, almonds, and golden raisins. Serve warm or at room temperature.

LEMON AND PARMESAN VEGETABLE MEDLEY

THESE VEGETABLES go together so well and are lovely to use any time of year. In the summer I grill the vegetables in large pieces, then cut them up and toss them with the lemon-Parmesan dressing. (See grilling variation below.) Any other time of year they are easy to make on a sheet pan. I love to keep them in my fridge and serve them cold, wrapped in warm flatbread with a little triple cream cheese, like Saint-André, for a glorious sandwich.

And while they are tasty enough to be a side dish on their own, they also add flavor to other recipes, including the Veggie and Black Bean Tostadas (page 125).

MAKES

6 TO 8 SERVINGS,
5 CUPS VEGGIES

HANDS-ON TIME

20 MINUTES

TOTAL TIME

50 MINUTES

1 teaspoon lemon zest

¼ cup fresh lemon juice

1¼ teaspoons kosher salt, divided

¾ teaspoon ground black pepper, divided

½ cup grated Parmesan

5 tablespoons extra-virgin olive oil, divided

1 yellow squash, cut into ½- to 1-inch pieces

1 zucchini, cut into ½- to 1-inch pieces

½ pint grape tomatoes

1 bell pepper, seeded and cut into ½- to 1-inch pieces

1 small red onion, sliced root to tip

1. Heat oven to 425°F. Make lemon-Parmesan dressing: In a medium bowl, whisk together lemon zest, lemon juice, ¼ teaspoon salt, ¼ teaspoon pepper, Parmesan, and 3 tablespoons olive oil; set aside.

2. Toss veggies in remaining 2 tablespoons olive oil, 1 teaspoon salt, and ½ teaspoon pepper. Roast until tender and charred in places, about 30 minutes.

3. Toss veggies with ½ tablespoon reserved dressing. Serve with extra dressing on the side.

GRILLING OPTION: Slice the zucchini and yellow squash lengthwise into strips. Cut the bell peppers into large pieces. Thread tomatoes and onion slices onto skewers. Brush vegetables with olive oil, season with salt and pepper, and grill over medium-high heat, until marked and tender, about 10 minutes, turning occasionally. Let cool slightly, and then cut into ½- to 1-inch pieces and continue with step 3 above.

crispy smashed potatoes with orange zest chimichurri

MAKES

4 TO 6 SERVINGS

HANDS-ON TIME

15 MINUTES

TOTAL TIME

1 HOUR

I'M NOT SAYING that I've eaten an entire batch of these potatoes before, but I'm not not saying that either. Crispy, buttery, fresh citrus, and herb-loaded heaven on a plate. Yes, they are that good!

1½ pounds red or white baby potatoes

¾ teaspoon kosher salt

3 tablespoons finely grated Asiago or Parmesan

4 tablespoons olive oil, divided

1 recipe Pistachio and Orange Chimichurri (below), prepared

1. Heat oven to 425°F. In a large pot, cover potatoes with water and salt, and bring to a boil. Reduce heat and simmer until tender, 8 to 10 minutes. Drain.
2. Drizzle a rimmed baking sheet with 3 tablespoons oil and transfer potatoes to baking sheet. Roll potatoes around to coat with oil.
3. Use the bottom of a glass or a strong spatula to smash the potatoes to about ½-inch thick. Sprinkle with cheese and drizzle with remaining oil.
4. Bake until golden and crisped around the edges, 18 to 20 minutes.
5. Serve hot, drizzled with some of the Pistachio and Orange Chimichurri. Serve remaining chimichurri on the side.

PISTACHIO AND ORANGE CHIMICHURRI

MAKES

1 CUP

HANDS-ON TIME

15 MINUTES

TOTAL TIME

20 MINUTES

CHIMICHURRIS AND GREMOLATA are two of my favorite herb condiments. Gremolata is an Italian parsley and garlic mixture with lemon zest, while chimichurri heralds from South America and blends herbs, garlic, olive oil, and vinegar. My herby mixture sort of blends the two and is delicious as a dip on snack boards, with burrata, or as a sauce for meat or chicken.

⅓ cup roasted and salted shelled pistachios

¼ teaspoon kosher salt

1 teaspoon orange zest

2 cloves garlic

2 cups lightly packed flat-leaf parsley

3 tablespoons fresh orange juice

¼ cup extra-virgin olive oil

1. Add pistachios, salt, zest, garlic, and parsley to a food processor and pulse until parsley is very finely chopped. Add orange juice and olive oil. Pulse until just combined and a pesto-like sauce is formed.
2. Let sit 10 to 20 minutes for flavors to meld. Serve or store, refrigerated, in an airtight container up to 5 days.

sage-roasted parsnips with hazelnuts and pomegranate

MAKES

6 TO 8 SERVINGS

HANDS-ON TIME

15 MINUTES

TOTAL TIME

1 HOUR 10 MINUTES

THERE ARE ONLY a few things my mother doesn't like to eat, and parsnips are on that list. For that obvious reason, I didn't grow up eating them.

I love parsnips now, and have spent years trying to convince my mom of their sweet, rooty goodness. My efforts are futile. Even the caramelized tips and soft creamy insides of these sage-roasted parsnips aren't enough to woo her taste buds into submission. For me, they are perfect, and the fresh burst of pomegranate is just icing on the cake.

TARA'S TIP

To remove the dark skin from hazelnuts, toast them in a 350°F oven for 6 to 7 minutes until they are hot and fragrant. Transfer to a clean kitchen towel and roll them up. Rub them vigorously in the towel; the friction and steam will help release the skin. If a little skin is left on the nuts, that is totally fine.

2 pounds parsnips, peeled

4 tablespoons olive oil, divided

1 teaspoon kosher salt

½ teaspoon ground black pepper

2 tablespoons minced sage, divided

¼ cup plain bread crumbs

⅓ cup finely grated Pecorino Romano

⅓ cup skinned hazelnuts, toasted and crushed

⅓ cup pomegranate arils

1. Heat oven to 400°F. Cut parsnips lengthwise into ¾- to 1-inch strips. On a rimmed baking sheet, toss parsnips with 2 tablespoons olive oil, salt, pepper, and 1 tablespoon sage.
2. Roast until tender and charred in parts, about 40 minutes.
3. While parsnips are roasting, combine the remaining 2 tablespoons olive oil, bread crumbs, and Pecorino on a small sheet pan and toast on a separate shelf in the oven, until just golden, 4 to 6 minutes.
4. In a small bowl, combine hazelnuts, pomegranate arils, and remaining 1 tablespoon sage.
5. When the parsnips are done, serve, topped with the bread crumbs and hazelnut mixture.

green beans with browned-butter almonds, garlic, and mint

MAKES

6 TO 8 SERVINGS

HANDS-ON TIME

15 MINUTES

TOTAL TIME

15 MINUTES

I LOVE THE RICHNESS browned butter gives to the almonds as they toast, and the garlic makes them so savory and good. Fresh mint adds a burst of amazing fresh flavor. If you're making this in the fall or for the holidays, swap the mint for loads of fresh, chopped flat-leaf parsley. I use haricots verts, which are thin green beans, but you can also use regular green beans. They are chubbier, so cook them an extra minute to get them tender.

4 tablespoons (½ stick) unsalted butter	1 pound trimmed haricots verts or regular green beans
½ cup sliced almonds	1 teaspoon kosher salt
2 cloves garlic, thinly sliced	½ teaspoon ground black pepper
	3 tablespoons chopped mint

1. Melt butter in a large skillet over medium-high heat. Add almonds. Stir occasionally until almonds begin to turn brown and the milk solids in the butter turn brown, 5 to 6 minutes.

2. Add the garlic and cover with the haricot verts, salt, and pepper. Reduce heat to medium, cover pan with a lid or foil, and steam 3 minutes. Uncover and cook, stirring, until beans are just tender, about 5 minutes.

3. Stir in mint and serve. Top with extra mint if desired.

grilled-pineapple and coconut rice

MAKES

6 TO 8 SERVINGS

HANDS-ON TIME

15 MINUTES

TOTAL TIME

55 MINUTES

THIS COCONUTTY and savory side dish is based on a coastal Columbian recipe with Caribbean influences and is delightful with grilled or braised chicken. Try it with my Pork Tenderloin with Adobo-Lime Glaze (page 113), salad, and fish. I serve it at gatherings with my Cuban Garlic-Lime Carnitas with Mojo (page 166), paired with plantains or tortilla chips. If it's summertime, grill your pineapple for a delightfully smoky flavor. In the colder months, I broil the pineapple to get a little caramelized char.

½ pineapple, rind removed	¼ teaspoon kosher salt
2 cups long-grain rice, uncooked	1 tablespoon fresh lime juice
1¾ cups coconut milk	5 mint leaves, chopped, plus more for garnish
¼ cup water	
2 teaspoons grated ginger	

TARA'S TIP

Leftovers of this rice make an amazing snack or dessert. Serve cold or warm with whole milk or half-and-half poured over it. A sprinkling of honey or sugar is a bonus. It's like an easy version of rice pudding, and a tasty treat.

1. Heat broiler to high. Slice pineapple into wedges and, if broiling, place on a foil-lined pan. Broil, turning once, until just charred in parts and heated through, 10 to 15 minutes. Alternatively, grill over medium-high heat until charred and warm. Remove pineapple to a cutting board and let it rest until cool enough to handle. Cut into ¼-inch dice. Set aside.

2. In a medium saucepan over medium-high heat, combine rice, coconut milk, water, ginger, and salt. Bring to a boil. Reduce heat to low, cover and cook until rice is tender and liquid is absorbed, 15 to 20 minutes.

3. Remove from heat and let rest uncovered 5 minutes.

4. Stir in lime juice, mint leaves, and pineapple. Serve, garnished with extra mint if desired.

MAKES

6 TO 8 SERVINGS,
ABOUT 10 CUPS

HANDS-ON TIME

45 MINUTES

TOTAL TIME

45 MINUTES

favorite corn succotash

AS A RECIPE developer, I take liberties, and I took one creating my version of succotash. It is my absolute favorite, and a side dish staple for anything grilled at my house.

Succotash originated as a seasonal corn stew from the Native Americans. It was made with fresh or dried corn and whatever veggies were in season—beans, squash, or pumpkin. Most ingredients were things Europeans had never seen.

From the northern settlers to the southern states, the versions have morphed and changed; everyone has their opinion of what belongs in a succotash.

For me, bacon, bell peppers, and cream are complete necessities alongside the corn. I suggest you make this once as written, then follow my tips and make it your own.

½ cup heavy cream

1½ cups green beans, cut into ½- to 1-inch pieces

12 ounces bacon, cut into ½-inch pieces

1 red bell pepper, cut into ½-inch pieces

6 large ears of fresh corn, corn cut from cobs (about 4½ cups)

1 bunch scallions, white and green parts sliced

1½ teaspoons kosher salt

1. In a small saucepan over medium-high heat, bring cream to a simmer. Maintain simmer 3 to 4 minutes, until cream is reduced by one-third. Remove from heat and set aside.

2. In a large skillet, bring 2 cups water to a boil. Add ½ teaspoon salt and the green beans and cook until just bright green, about 3 minutes. Drain and set aside.

3. In the same skillet, cook bacon over medium heat until crisp, stirring frequently, 5 to 7 minutes. Drain, reserving fat in a bowl, and set bacon aside.

4. Add a few teaspoons of the bacon fat back to the skillet and sauté the red peppers over medium-high heat until just tender, about 2 minutes. Add the green beans, corn, and scallions and cook, stirring, until everything is just heated through, about 4 minutes.

5. Add the bacon, salt, and reduced cream and remove from heat. Serve hot or warm.

TARA'S TIP

This recipe is very flexible in proportions and ingredients. You can add, eliminate, or substitute most ingredients to your taste. For example, you might substitute frozen lima beans for the green beans. Or add some diced summer squash or ocra. In winter, use frozen corn and add cubed squash.

LOOKS DELICIOUS When dicing and chopping your vegetables, work to make pieces uniform in size—about the size of a few kernels of corn. Not only does it look pretty, but you'll get flavor in each bite.

WEEKNIGHT ROUTINES

thai meatball golden coconut curry

MAKES

6 TO 8 SERVINGS

HANDS-ON TIME

45 MINUTES

TOTAL TIME

1 HOUR

THIS ONE-PAN coconut curry is easy to pull together with some spices from the pantry and a few fresh veggies. The Thai meatballs make this meal extraordinary, and leftovers are rare at my house.

The full-fat coconut milk gives the dish a subtle sweetness and creates a quick, rich sauce that's perfect for spooning over rice. The turmeric gives it a luscious gold color and aromatic flavor. Add a few tiny slices of fresh red cayenne chilis for a kick of heat.

2 tablespoons olive oil

1 teaspoon fennel seeds

1 red or yellow bell pepper, cut into 2-inch strips

1 small red onion, sliced root to tip

1 clove garlic, minced

1 cup grape tomatoes, cut in half

½ teaspoon turmeric

¾ teaspoon dried basil

¼ teaspoon cayenne

½ teaspoon kosher salt

1 cup water

1 recipe Thai Chicken Meatballs (page 96), prepared

1 (14.5-ounce) can coconut milk

Chopped cilantro

Sliced red chilis, like fresh cayenne (optional)

Cooked long-grain rice, for serving

1. Heat 2 tablespoons oil in a large nonstick skillet or pot over medium-high heat. Add fennel seeds, bell pepper, and onion and cook 3 minutes.

2. Stir in garlic, tomatoes, turmeric, basil, cayenne, salt, and water and bring to a simmer. Cook until liquid is reduced by half, 6 to 7 minutes.

3. Add meatballs and coconut milk to pan. Stir sauce gently and bring to a simmer, cooking until meatballs are heated through. Serve with rice and garnish with cilantro and sliced chilis, if desired.

TARA'S TIP

This curry is delicious with more than just meatballs. Try it with sliced chicken breast or shrimp. I cut the chicken into thin strips so it cooks in about the same time it would take the meatballs to heat through. For a vegetarian option, add a few cups of your favorite cut-up veggies in place of the meatballs and use soy sauce in place of fish sauce.

LOOKS DELICIOUS To make this curry photo-worthy, use lots of bright fresh cilantro and spicy chilis.

thai meatball lettuce wraps with sweet chili sauce

THESE WILL BE on regular dinner rotation once your crew tastes the crisp lettuce wrapped around a savory filling bursting with Thai flavor. They're a great way to eat salad, right out of your hand. The tender meatballs add so much flavor that the only dressing you need is a squeeze of lime and a drizzle of sweet chili sauce.

TARA'S TIP

Sweet chili sauce is made from red chilis, spices, vinegar, and sugar. It's great served over the meatballs in these lettuce wraps or as a dipping sauce, but you should also try it on seafood or in place of ketchup on burgers. You'll be hooked!

1 recipe Thai Chicken Meatballs (page 96), prepared

1 cup julienned or shredded carrots

1 small red or yellow bell pepper, julienned to 1-inch pieces

1 cup sliced cucumbers

2 scallions, white and green parts sliced

2 small heads Butter or Boston lettuce, leaves separated

2 cups cooked short-grain sushi rice

½ cup chopped cilantro, plus more for garnish

½ cup cashews, coarsely chopped

Sweet chili sauce

Lime wedges

1. In a medium bowl toss together carrots, bell peppers, cilantro, cucumber, and scallions.
2. To serve: Top a lettuce leaf with a spoonful of rice, 2 or 3 warm meatballs, and some of the vegetable mixture, extra cilantro, and cashews. Drizzle with chili sauce and a squeeze of lime.

MAKES

ABOUT 30
MEATBALLS

HANDS-ON TIME

25 MINUTES

TOTAL TIME

35 MINUTES

thai chicken meatballs

AUTHENTIC THAI meals typically create a delectable balance of four main flavors: salty, sweet, sour, and spicy. Pungent herbs and salty fish sauce mix with sweet flavors like ginger and tangy acids.

I've kept the Thai flavors but created a mild version of these meatballs, so they can be used in any number of dishes. They are such a hit with my family, I often double the batch and keep some in the freezer.

I use the meatballs like I would plain chicken—over rice, with noodles, in a stir-fry or a curry, on a sandwich, or in lettuce wraps. Add any sauce you like depending on what you have in the pantry—a simple soy glaze, sweet chili sauce right out of the bottle, or my Thai Peanut Sauce (page 143).

1 small yellow onion, roughly chopped

1 clove garlic

2 teaspoons fresh grated ginger

1 jalapeño, seeded

1¾ pounds boneless, skinless chicken breasts, cut into pieces

½ cup packed cilantro

1 tablespoon fish sauce

½ cup plain bread crumbs

2 egg whites

1. In a food processor, combine onion, garlic, ginger, and jalapeño and pulse until finely chopped. Add chicken, cilantro, fish sauce, and bread crumbs and pulse until well blended but not quite puréed; no large pieces of chicken should remain. Add egg whites and pulse briefly.

2. Heat broiler to high and place rack 4 inches from heat. Line a baking sheet with foil and lightly coat with cooking spray.

3. Use a 2-tablespoon cookie scoop or a ⅛ cup to portion mixture into about 30 balls. Coat hands with water and shape into meatballs. Arrange on prepared baking sheet.

4. Broil until meatballs are lightly browned, about 4 minutes. Turn meatballs over and broil another 4 minutes. Serve, or continue to add them to another recipe.

STOVETOP VARIATION: To cook meatballs on the stovetop, heat 2 tablespoons olive oil in a large nonstick skillet over medium-high heat. Cook meatballs in batches, turning occasionally, until cooked through, about 6 minutes.

FROZEN VARIATION: If you've doubled the meatball recipe and have some in the freezer, heat oven to 350°F. Cook frozen meatballs until the internal temperature on a meat thermometer reads 170°F, about 30 minutes.

yogurt-marinated grilled chicken

THE TANGY yogurt marinade in this recipe is magic at imparting flavor and acid to make the chicken perfectly tender, flavorful, and oh-so-versatile. You can serve the chicken on its own, in a sandwich, on top of a salad, or even in kebab form.

MAKES

4 TO 6 SERVINGS,
1 CUP MARINADE

HANDS-ON TIME

20 MINUTES

TOTAL TIME

4 HOURS

1 tablespoon minced garlic

¾ cup plain whole-fat yogurt

2 tablespoons olive oil

1 tablespoon Dijon mustard

2 tablespoons fresh lemon juice

2 teaspoons kosher salt

1 teaspoon ground coriander

¼ teaspoon ground black pepper

1½ pounds boneless, skinless chicken breasts

1. In a large bowl, combine garlic, yogurt, olive oil, mustard, lemon juice, salt, coriander, and pepper. Add chicken, cover with plastic wrap, and chill 1 to 4 hours.

2. When ready to cook, heat grill to medium-high. Remove chicken, discarding marinade. Grill, turning once, until just cooked through, 4 to 5 minutes per side.

KEBABS VARIATION: To make kebabs, cut chicken into 1-inch cubes and add to marinade before chilling. Soak bamboo skewers in water for 20 minutes to prevent them from burning when grilled. Thread chicken and desired veggies or fruit on skewers and grill over medium heat, turning occasionally, until cooked through, 10 to 12 minutes.

chicken and biscuits with honey butter

FOR A WEEKNIGHT DINNER that comes together in the time it takes to grill chicken and make a batch of biscuits, look no further. There's no need to batter and fry chicken for my take on a Southern classic. Simply slather a biscuit with honey butter and top it with thin slices of grilled chicken and a tangy slaw.

Making baking powder biscuits was one of my dinner jobs growing up. I would cut the butter into the flour mixture with a pastry blender. Then I'd gently stir in the liquid and pat the dough out on a flour-dusted board. I loved baking the little scraps for taste tests. Now, I love making biscuits as big as my hand and filling them with honey butter and Southern goodness.

MAKES

6 BISCUIT SANDWICHES

HANDS-ON TIME

35 MINUTES

TOTAL TIME

35 MINUTES, NOT INCLUDING BISCUIT AND CHICKEN PREPARATION

---

6 Mile-High Buttermilk Biscuits (page 43), prepared

1 recipe Yogurt-Marinated Grilled Chicken (page 97), prepared

3 tablespoons mayonnaise

3 tablespoons sour cream

2 teaspoons Dijon mustard

1 teaspoon apple cider vinegar

2 cups slaw mix or finely sliced cabbage

¼ cup chopped flat-leaf parsley

Salt and pepper, to taste

3 tablespoons honey

½ cup (1 stick) butter, softened

Pinch cayenne pepper

1. Prepare the slaw topping: In a medium bowl, whisk together mayonnaise, sour cream, mustard, and cider vinegar. Toss with slaw mix and parsley, then season with salt and pepper to taste; set aside.

2. Make honey butter: In a small bowl, combine honey, butter, and cayenne with an electric mixer on low speed until smooth.

3. Assemble sandwiches: Split biscuits in half and spread the bottom half with honey butter, top with sliced chicken, slaw, and top half of biscuit.

TARA'S TIP

The sandwich is delicious with either warm, just-grilled chicken or cold, leftover chicken. If you're in a hurry, shred a rotisserie chicken instead.

To make your own slaw mix, combine 1½ cups finely sliced cabbage, ½ cup sliced red cabbage, and ½ cup shredded carrot.

MAKES

4 SERVINGS

HANDS-ON TIME

15 MINUTES

TOTAL TIME

25 MINUTES,
NOT INCLUDING
CHICKEN
MARINATING

TARA'S TIP

Soak bamboo skewers in water for about 20 minutes before using so they don't burn on the grill.

chicken mango kebabs with chickpea chutney vinaigrette

CHICKPEA VINAIGRETTE? You bet. You can call it a chickpea sauce if you'd like, but it's a delicious change from the norm to eat with a grilled meal. I use my delicious yogurt-marinated chicken to make these kebabs and just cut the chicken into pieces before marinating. The small pieces only take a few minutes to cook on the grill—just enough time for the mango to get charred and juicy.

2 tablespoons Major Grey's Chutney

1 tablespoon water

1 tablespoon apple cider vinegar

1 tablespoon canola or avocado oil

½ cup drained, canned chickpeas

1 tablespoon chopped flat-leaf parsley, plus more for garnish

1 mango, peeled and cut into 1-inch pieces

1 recipe Kebab Variation for Yogurt-Marinated Grilled Chicken (page 97), prepared up to grilling stage

Bamboo or metal skewers

1. For the chickpea vinaigrette: In a medium bowl, whisk together chutney, water, vinegar, and oil. Stir in chickpeas and parsley; set aside.
2. For the kebabs: When ready to cook, heat grill to medium heat. Thread marinated chicken cubes onto skewers, alternating with pieces of mango. Grill, turning occasionally, until chicken is cooked through, 10 to 12 minutes.
3. Drizzle vinaigrette over grilled kebabs, garnish with parsley, and serve.

spice-rubbed steak with avocado smash

MAKES

4 SERVINGS

HANDS-ON TIME

10 MINUTES

TOTAL TIME

30 MINUTES

A TANGY AND FRESH avocado smash replaces the typical compound butter steak topping used in a French bistro. I suggest serving the steaks with a hearty side of fries from the freezer section of the store. Cook them in the oven and season with plenty of salt and pepper for easy, classic steak frites!

A 6-ounce serving is great for the average dinner eater, but if you're a big steak eater, you may want to double the portion. It's easy to double, or triple, since the divine spice rub is already prepared.

2 (12-ounce) thick-cut New York strip steaks	3 scallions, white and green parts chopped
2 tablespoons Go-To Steak Rub (below), divided	2 tablespoons rice wine vinegar
2 ripe avocados	¼ teaspoon kosher salt
	½ teaspoon ground black pepper

1. Rub each steak all over with 1 tablespoon steak rub. Let steaks sit at room temperature 15 minutes. Heat grill to medium-high.
2. While steaks rest, in a medium bowl, mash avocados with scallions, vinegar, salt, and pepper; set aside.
3. Grill steaks, turning once, to medium-rare (135°F on an instant-read thermometer), 5 to 6 minutes per side. Transfer steaks to a cutting board and let them rest 2 minutes.
4. Cut steaks in half to serve 4. Top with avocado smash and serve with fries, if desired.

GO-TO STEAK RUB

MAKES

7 TABLESPOONS

HANDS-ON TIME

5 MINUTES

TOTAL TIME

5 MINUTES

THIS RUB IS A STAPLE in my pantry, and it's not just for steak! It can go on roasts, burgers, or chicken on the grill or in the multi-cooker. I also use it on my Herb-Glazed Fall-Off-the-Bone BBQ Ribs (page 172). When I do use it on steaks, my rule of thumb is to rub 1 to 1½ teaspoons all over a 12-ounce steak. Allow the steaks to sit at room temperature 10 to 20 minutes before grilling to soak in all the flavorful goodness. When I'm making ribs, I use 3 tablespoons for each rack of ribs before cooking.

2 tablespoons chili powder	1 teaspoon ground black pepper
4 teaspoons sweet paprika	2 teaspoons onion powder
4 teaspoons kosher salt	4 teaspoons ground coriander
½ teaspoon ground cinnamon	

Combine spices in small bowl and store mixture in a sealed container up to 6 months.

WEEKNIGHT ROUTINES

103

MAKES

4 TO 6 SERVINGS

HANDS-ON TIME

25 MINUTES

TOTAL TIME

25 MINUTES

tomato and roquefort steak flatbread

I'LL TAKE ANY EXCUSE to eat this delicious flatbread with steak and blue cheese. The classic combo of piquant, creamy cheese and perfectly spiced steak is made even better with fresh tomatoes and peppery arugula.

Flank steak is easy to grill, and you can even broil it when your grill is covered for winter. Swap it for other quick-cooking steaks if you'd like—skirt steak, rib eye, and New York strip are great options.

1 (16-ounce) flank steak	Pinch ground black pepper
4 teaspoons Go-To Steak Rub (page 103)	1 pint grape tomatoes
¾ cup Roquefort cheese, crumbled and divided	Bamboo or metal skewers
	4 naan-style flatbreads or small baked pizza crusts
¼ cup heavy cream	2 cups baby arugula

1. Rub steak all over with steak rub. Let sit at room temperature 15 minutes. Heat grill to medium-high.

2. In a medium bowl, mash ½ cup of the Roquefort cheese with the heavy cream and a pinch of pepper; set aside.

3. Thread grape tomatoes on skewers and grill alongside steak until just charred. Set aside while steak cooks.

4. Grill steak, turning once, until cooked to medium (140°F on an instant-read thermometer), 6 to 7 minutes per side. Remove to a cutting board. Let rest 2 minutes, then slice steak across the grain.

5. While steak rests, grill flatbreads on one side until marked, 1 minute or less. Spread grilled sides with cheese mixture. Top with sliced steak and tomatoes. Sprinkle with remaining crumbled cheese and arugula to serve.

TARA'S TIP

If you aren't a fan of blue cheese, swap it for a Brie or a triple cream like Saint-André. Use a mild goat cheese, or be even more straight-forward and melt shredded Monterey Jack or Gouda on the flatbread before adding the steak and toppings.

Soak bamboo skewers in water for about 20 minutes before using so they don't burn on the grill.

jalapeño cornmeal waffles with carnitas and crema

MAKES

6 TO 8 SERVINGS

HANDS-ON TIME

35 MINUTES

TOTAL TIME

45 MINUTES, NOT INCLUDING CARNITAS PREPARATION

I LOVE THE TREND of food trucks and food-truck gatherings all over the country. The creative concoctions these budding chefs share, right out of the back of a truck, is amazing.

Perhaps the idea for this recipe came from visiting a waffle truck and then a taco stand, but it got my creative juices going. These mini waffles—a variation of my breakfast Cornmeal Waffles (page 187)—get a delicious dinner makeover. Use my Garlic-Lime Carnitas or any leftover pulled pork to make this fun meal.

Make your own crema by whisking together ½ cup sour cream and 2 teaspoons lime juice.

JALAPEÑO CORNMEAL WAFFLES

1¼ cups all-purpose flour

¾ cup yellow cornmeal

¼ cup light brown sugar

1 tablespoon baking powder

½ teaspoon baking soda

½ teaspoon salt

2 large eggs

1 cup low-fat buttermilk

½ teaspoon vanilla extract

¼ cup canola oil

4 tablespoons butter, melted

2 medium jalapeños, seeded and finely diced

¾ cup grated sharp cheddar cheese

TOPPINGS

1 recipe Cuban Garlic-Lime Carnitas with Mojo (page 166), prepared

2 cups shredded red cabbage or slaw mix

Crema

Chopped cilantro

Radishes, thinly sliced

Lime wedges

TARA'S TIP

I like this recipe with a bold, flavorful cheese and keep bags of shredded sharp cheddar in the fridge to save on prep time. If you don't grate your own, Tillamook has thick-cut shreds that I love. The thick pieces of tangy cheddar shine through as they melt perfectly into the crevices of the waffles.

1. In a large bowl, whisk together flour, cornmeal, sugar, baking powder, baking soda, and salt. In a separate bowl, whisk together eggs, buttermilk, vanilla, oil, and butter. Add egg mixture to flour mixture and whisk well to combine. Stir in jalapeño and cheddar.

2. Heat oven to 200°F. Heat waffle iron and spoon about 2 tablespoons batter into the center of each mold. Cook until baked through and just turning golden, about 2 to 2½ minutes, depending on your iron. Waffles will be about 3 inches in diameter. Place waffles in warm oven while you cook the rest.

3. Top waffles with warm Cuban Garlic-Lime Carnitas, cabbage, and crema. Garnish with cilantro, radish slices, and a squeeze of lime.

LOOKS DELICIOUS For a fun presentation, serve these waffles like a taco bar, setting out the waffles and all the fixings and letting everyone build their own.

garlic-lime carnitas totchos

HAD TOTCHOS (nachos made with tater tots instead of chips) been a part of my childhood, they would have been a favorite for sure! The crunchy tots are brilliant topped with all sorts of delicious fixings. I love using my Cuban Garlic-Lime Carnitas or even grilled chicken or steak. Prepare the carnitas in advance on a weekend or for a party. Reheat the leftovers to make this meal fast.

1 (32-ounce) package frozen tater tots

PINEAPPLE SALSA

¼ pineapple, cut into a small dice

3 tablespoons scallions, white and green parts chopped

2 tablespoons fresh lime juice

¼ cup chopped cilantro, plus more for garnish

TOPPINGS

1 recipe Cuban Garlic-Lime Carnitas with Mojo (page 166), prepared and reheated if made in advance

¾ cup crumbled cotija cheese

Restaurant-Style Salsa (page 39)

Diced avocados

Sliced jalapeños

1. Cook tater tots according to package directions.
2. While tots cook, make pineapple salsa: In a small bowl, stir together diced pineapple, scallions, lime juice, and cilantro; set aside.
3. To serve, divide tater tots between each plate and top with warm Cuban Garlic-Lime Carnitas. Top with cotija, pineapple salsa, Restaurant-Style Salsa, avocados, and jalapeños. Garnish with cilantro.

TARA'S TIP

If you're reheating previously prepared Garlic-Lime Carnitas, put the shredded pork in a covered saucepan with some of the mojo juices or chicken broth. Cook over medium-high heat until just heated through.

adobo-lime chicken and summer melon salad

MAKES

4 SERVINGS

HANDS-ON TIME

40 MINUTES

TOTAL TIME

2 HOURS
40 MINUTES

A QUICK MARINADE gives chicken the boost it needs to get out of the weeknight dinner rut. A delightfully intense combo of soy, vinegar, and lime juice is perfect with fresh, sweet melon, the sharp flavors of feta, and summery mint.

When melon isn't in season, use tropical fruit such as mango or pineapple, or a thinly sliced apple.

1 recipe Adobo-Lime Marinade (below), prepared

4 small boneless, skinless chicken breasts

2 tablespoons light brown sugar

½ cup chopped pistachios

½ cup crumbled feta cheese

¼ cup coarsely chopped mint

4 cups thinly sliced melon (watermelon, honeydew, and cantaloupe)

1. Pour marinade over chicken breasts in a large resealable bag. Seal bag and marinate in refrigerator 2 to 5 hours.
2. Heat grill to medium-high. Remove chicken, reserving marinade, and grill until just cooked through (165°F on an instant-read thermometer), 5 to 7 minutes on each side.
3. Meanwhile, add reserved marinade to a small saucepan, along with the brown sugar. Bring to a simmer over medium heat and cook until mixture is slightly reduced and like a glaze, 4 to 5 minutes. (Boiling the marinade kills the bacteria from the raw meat.) Brush grilled chicken with glaze.
4. Slice chicken and arrange it over watermelon, honeydew, and cantaloupe. Sprinkle with pistachios, feta, and mint and serve with extra adobo glaze.

ADOBO-LIME MARINADE

MAKES

4 SERVINGS

HANDS-ON TIME

15 MINUTES

TOTAL TIME

15 MINUTES

YOU MAY HAVE HEARD the term "adobo" in reference to Mexican flavors and foods. It's a wonderful dried chili-based paste used for a million things. This adobo has Filipino roots and is a concentrated flavor base with soy sauce and garlic.

⅓ cup low-sodium soy sauce

3 large garlic cloves

½ teaspoon dried oregano

¼ cup water

¼ cup apple cider vinegar

1 teaspoon lime zest

2 tablespoons fresh lime juice

In a blender, combine all ingredients. Blend until smooth. Refrigerate in airtight container until ready to use, up to 2 days. Shake well before using.

pork tenderloin with adobo-lime glaze

PORK TENDERLOIN is one of my go-to, speedy dinners because it's a tender, quick-cooking meat that I can season to suit any taste. Based on a Filipino adobo flavor, this marinated variation goes with just about any side or salad. I love it with grilled or roasted vegetables or my Grilled-Pineapple and Coconut Rice (page 86). You may want to make two, because the second you start slicing this, pieces disappear off the cutting board in a hurry.

1 recipe Adobo-Lime Marinade (page 111), prepared

1 (16-ounce) pork tenderloin

2 tablespoons light brown sugar

Lime wedges

Cilantro

1. Pour marinade over pork in a large resealable bag. Seal bag and marinate in refrigerator 2 to 5 hours.
2. Heat grill to medium-high. Remove pork, reserving marinade, and grill tenderloins, turning occasionally, until cooked to medium-well (145°F on an instant-read thermometer), 15 to 20 minutes.
3. Meanwhile, add reserved marinade to a small saucepan, along with the brown sugar. Bring to a simmer over medium heat and cook until mixture is slightly reduced and like a glaze, 3 to 5 minutes. Brush tenderloin with glaze.
4. Serve sliced tenderloin with lime wedges, cilantro, and extra glaze on the side.

MAKES

4 SERVINGS

HANDS-ON TIME

30 MINUTES

TOTAL TIME

2 HOURS
30 MINUTES

TARA'S TIP

You can also roast the pork in a 400°F oven on a foil-lined baking sheet instead of grilling it. Turn it over after about 6 minutes. Continue to cook to medium-well (145°F on an instant-read thermometer), another 10 to 12 minutes.

MAKES

4 TO 6 SERVINGS

HANDS-ON TIME

25 MINUTES

TOTAL TIME

45 MINUTES

lemony chicken and charred-artichoke pasta

A HANDY, helpful, and always-delicious roast chicken is a weeknight meal time-saver. I make two at a time on a weekend (see Golden Roast Chickens with Pan Sauce, page 150), so I have one for midweek recipes. And if you don't cook on the weekend, those grocery store rotisserie chickens are perfect for making a quick dinner.

You'll only need a small portion of shredded, cooked chicken for this lemony pasta because I focused on getting in as many perfectly charred artichokes as possible. The cheesy croutons are a heavenly addition and bake while the pasta cooks, but if it's a busy night, use store-bought croutons or broken crostini.

TARA'S TIP

I used fresh egg fettuccine, which gives this dish a rich chew. If you can't find fresh pasta, dry works just as well.

Canned artichokes can be subbed for the frozen in a pinch. Dry artichokes on paper towels before cooking, and reduce the salt since the canned artichokes will be saturated with the canning brine.

PARMESAN CROUTONS

4 to 6 slices rustic bread, torn into 1-inch pieces (about 2 cups)

1 tablespoon unsalted butter, melted

1 tablespoon finely grated Parmesan

PASTA

12 ounces fresh egg fettuccine or dry fettuccine

2 tablespoons olive oil

1 (12-ounce) bag frozen artichoke hearts, thawed and drained

1 tablespoon unsalted butter

½ teaspoon kosher salt

2 small shallot, sliced root to tip

Zest from one lemon

¼ cup fresh lemon juice

¾ cup heavy cream

¾ cup finely grated Parmesan, divided

¼ cup water

1½ cups shredded cooked chicken (Golden Roast Chickens, page 150)

⅓ cup chopped flat-leaf parsley

1. Make Parmesan croutons: Heat oven to 400°F. On a rimmed baking sheet, toss bread pieces with melted butter and Parmesan and spread on pan in an even layer. Bake until just golden brown, about 10 minutes; set aside.

2. Cook pasta in very salty water according to package directions, drain.

3. In a cast-iron skillet or heavy-duty nonstick skillet, heat olive oil over medium-high heat. Add artichokes and cook until crispy on one side, 6 to 8 minutes. Turn the artichokes and cook until just heated through, about 2 more minutes. Remove artichokes from skillet and set aside.

4. Reduce heat to medium and add butter, salt, and shallots to the skillet. Cook 1 minute then add lemon zest and lemon juice. Cook 1 minute, until the lemon juice reduces and gets concentrated.

5. Stir in cream, ½ cup Parmesan, water, and reserved pasta. Cook, stirring, about 2 minutes, until cheese has melted and sauce is warmed through. Add artichokes and shredded chicken.

6. Serve immediately, topped with croutons, parsley, and the remaining Parmesan.

chicken pozole verde

MAKES

6 TO 8 SERVINGS,
8 CUPS

HANDS-ON TIME

25 MINUTES

TOTAL TIME

1 HOUR 10 MINUTES

THIS IS NOT your average chicken soup. It's one of my all-time favorites, and it relies on loads of tomatillos, charred chilis, spices, and hominy to create a traditional Mexican stew. This recipe is a fantastic way to use rotisserie or roasted chicken for a weeknight meal (see Golden Roast Chickens), and comes together in just a few steps.

It's imperative to roast the ingredients that make up the flavorful green base to get a smoky char. I roasted what felt like a million chilis to get just the right heat level and balance. The garlic mellows as it roasts so it's not overpowering. The results are beyond amazing!

1 medium yellow onion, peeled and cut into large pieces

3 tablespoons olive oil, divided

1 poblano pepper (about 6 inches in length)

1 jalapeño

1 pound tomatillos (about 6 medium), husks removed

4 cloves garlic, with skins on

¾ cup chopped celery, cut in half moons

3 (15-ounce) cans low-sodium chicken broth (5½ cups)

1 cup water

½ teaspoon dried oregano

1 teaspoon ground cumin

½ teaspoon ground coriander

1 teaspoon kosher salt

2 (15-ounce) cans hominy, drained

2 cups shredded cooked chicken (Golden Roast Chickens, page 150)

Toppings: cilantro, sliced radishes, avocado, sour cream, tortilla chips, and lime wedges

1. Heat broiler to high and arrange rack 4 to 6 inches from the heat. Line a rimmed baking sheet with foil. On the pan, toss onion slices with 1 tablespoon olive oil. Arrange onions, pepper, jalapeño, tomatillos, and garlic cloves on the pan. Broil, turning occasionally until peppers and tomatillos are charred and onions are softened, 8 to 10 minutes.

2. When cool enough to handle, remove skin and seeds from peppers and discard. Coarsely chop peppers. Remove husks from garlic cloves. Place garlic, peppers, onions, and tomatillos in a blender or food processor and pulse until finely chopped. Set aside.

3. In a large soup pot, heat 2 tablespoons olive oil over medium heat and add celery. Cook until just translucent and soft, about 5 minutes. Stir in the pulsed pepper mixture and cook until fragrant, about 2 minutes.

4. Add the chicken broth, water, oregano, cumin, coriander, and salt. Cook, stirring occasionally, until flavors have blended and onions and celery are very soft, about 20 minutes. Stir in the chicken and hominy.

5. Serve, garnished with your favorite toppings and a squeeze of lime.

TARA'S TIP

It's easy to mistake pasilla peppers and poblanos as they look similar and supermarkets often mislabel them. Pasillas are spicier than mild poblanos, so once you've roasted the base ingredients, taste the poblano pepper. If it's hot, it's a pasilla! Adjust the soup heat level based on how much of the roasted pepper you put in. Save any spicy leftovers for morning omelets or salsa.

FLAVOR-INSPIRED DINNERS

creamy cacio e pepe
with lemon arugula

MAKES

4 TO 6 SERVINGS

HANDS-ON TIME

15 MINUTES

TOTAL TIME

30 MINUTES

THE ITALIANS gifted the world with cacio e pepe—literally translated to "cheese and pepper"—and I'm just here to remind you about the goodness. Tart lemony dressing mixed with peppery arugula is an added bonus with the rich cheesiness.

This grown-up version of buttered noodles uses starchy pasta water, Pecorino Romano, and an almost obscene amount of cracked black pepper to create a glossy, flavorful dinner. Even with only a few ingredients, this recipe can be tricky and the cheese can clump. I've created a simpler version so everyone is successful the first time around! I call for a little heavy cream and butter (okay, a fair amount of butter) to make the sauce foolproof.

2 tablespoons fresh lemon juice	2 cups reserved pasta cooking-water
3 tablespoons extra-virgin olive oil	½ cup finely grated Parmesan
1 (16-ounce) package dry spaghetti	½ cup finely grated Pecorino Romano
⅓ cup unsalted butter	½ cup heavy cream
2½ teaspoons coarse-ground black pepper	3 cups baby arugula

1. In a small bowl, whisk together the lemon juice and olive oil; set aside.
2. Cook spaghetti in salty water according to package directions until al dente, or just cooked through. Reserve 2 cups of the pasta-cooking water and drain pasta. Return pot to stove over medium-high heat and add 1 cup of the pasta water.
3. Let the pasta water simmer until it is reduced by half, 4 to 5 minutes. Add butter and ground pepper and stir until butter is melted, about 2 minutes.
4. Remove from heat. Add pasta, cream, and cheese. Swirl with tongs to toss the pasta until well coated. Add tablespoons of additional pasta water, if needed, to reach a smooth, saucy consistency.
5. Toss arugula with reserved lemon juice and olive oil. Serve pasta immediately, topped with arugula and extra cheese.

TARA'S TIP

Cacio e pepe isn't meant to be a sauce-coated pasta like an alfredo, even though it has similar flavors. The sauce should be thin, and silky. The heavy cream helps prevent the cheese from clumping so don't substitute it with half-and-half or milk.

LOOKS DELICIOUS Pasta likes to soak up any liquid you give it, so serve this pasta immediately upon assembling. If it sits for a few minutes, it will absorb the sauce. Swirl in some of the reserved hot pasta water to bring it back.

FLAVOR-INSPIRED DINNERS

MAKES

4 TO 6 SERVINGS

HANDS-ON TIME

25 MINUTES

TOTAL TIME

45 MINUTES

marvelously easy thai peanut curry

TYPICALLY, blending and mincing all the delicious things to make a flavorful base for a fresh curry takes a lot of time. But with the magic of prepared curry paste, you can make a pretty authentic-tasting curry in about half an hour! Your grocery store most likely carries red curry paste, but if you're lucky enough to live by an Asian grocer, experiment with all the varieties they offer and find your favorite. (Some are more spicy or aromatic than others.) The addition of creamy peanut butter here adds a delicious American twist. It reminds me of the Massaman curry I get at the corner restaurant.

TARA'S TIP

The key to making this curry come together quickly is to have all the ingredients chopped, grated, and measured before cooking.

I use my microwave as a shortcut for steaming vegetables. Place them in a microwave-safe dish, add 1 tablespoon water, a pinch of salt, and cover the dish. Microwave for 6 to 8 minutes until they are just tender.

6 cups chopped vegetables, such as green beans, snow peas, cauliflower, bell peppers, and broccoli

2 tablespoons olive or avocado oil

1 medium yellow onion, cut into large dice

2 tablespoons grated ginger

1 clove garlic, minced

2 teaspoons fish sauce

2 tablespoons red curry paste

3 tablespoons creamy peanut butter

2 tablespoons fresh lime juice

1½ teaspoons kosher salt

1½ cups unsweetened coconut milk

2 cups low-sodium chicken or vegetable broth

Crushed peanuts

Fresh basil

2 cups long-grain rice, cooked

1. Steam vegetables until just tender. Set aside.
2. Make curry: In a large, nonstick skillet, over medium-high heat, heat olive oil. Add the onion, ginger, and garlic and cook until the onion is tender, about 5 minutes. Add the fish sauce, curry paste, peanut butter, lime juice, salt, coconut milk, and chicken broth. Cook, stirring until everything is combined and starts to simmer. Reduce heat to medium-low and simmer 1 minute. Add the vegetables and gently simmer another 4 to 5 minutes.
3. Serve over cooked rice and top with chopped peanuts and fresh basil.

LOOKS DELICIOUS This quick curry is easy to customize. I usually make it with all vegetables, but you can use your own mix of veggies and even add tofu, shrimp, or chicken.

veggie and black bean tostadas

MAYBE IT'S meatless Monday at your house, or maybe you just love Southwest flavors as much as I do. These tostadas use the same vegetable medley as my Lemon and Parmesan Vegetable Medley but with the addition of spice, sweet potato, and black beans. Serve on crispy shells for a fun change or use the filling for vegetarian tacos.

MAKES

6 TO 8 SERVINGS

HANDS-ON TIME

40 MINUTES

TOTAL TIME

1 HOUR

1 recipe Lemon and Parmesan Vegetable Medley (page 79), prepared with ½ teaspoon chili powder and ½ teaspoon ground cumin added to dressing

1 tablespoon olive oil

½ large sweet potato, peeled and cut into ½-inch pieces

¾ cup canned black beans, drained

¼ cup sour cream

1 tablespoon fresh lime juice

8 corn tostada shells

8 ounces Monterey Jack cheese, shredded (2 cups)

½ cup chopped cilantro

1. While the Lemon and Parmesan Vegetable Medley is cooking, spread sweet potatoes on a rimmed baking sheet and toss with olive oil. Roast with vegetables in a 425°F oven until tender, about 15 minutes.

2. In a large bowl, toss roasted sweet potatoes with Lemon and Parmesan Vegetable Medley and black beans; set aside.

3. Sprinkle cheese on tostada shells and melt in warm oven. When cheese is melted, use a spatula to remove tortillas to a serving platter or plates.

4. In a small bowl, whisk together sour cream with lime juice until smooth.

5. Top cheese-covered tostadas with vegetable mixture, lime sour cream, and chopped cilantro.

TARA'S TIP

Making your own tostada shells is easy if you can't find them at the store. Simply fill the bottom of a medium saucepan with half-inch of vegetable or avocado oil. Heat on medium-high until very hot. Fry corn tortillas, one at a time, until crisp. Drain on paper towels.

orange-ginger pork dumplings

MAKES

35 DUMPLINGS

HANDS-ON TIME

1 HOUR

TOTAL TIME

1 HOUR

I LOVE THAT my job allows me play in the kitchen. A while back, I was experimenting with food-grade essential oils and, just for fun, added a little cilantro oil to my dumpling filling and orange oil to the dipping sauce. I loved the incredible pops of flavor!

For everyday cooks, there's no need to use essential oils, you can use fresh ingredients. Using orange zest in the sauce imparts the same oils and flavor and is a marvelous twist on a standard dumpling dip.

3 shiitake mushrooms, cleaned and coarsely chopped (about ½ cup)

1 heaping teaspoon freshly chopped ginger

2 cloves garlic

1 cup store-bought slaw mix

1½ teaspoons sesame oil

2 tablespoons rice wine vinegar

2 tablespoons fresh orange juice

¼ cup chopped cilantro

¼ cup chopped scallions

3 links sweet Italian sausage, casings removed (6½ ounces)

35 (3-inch-square) wonton wrappers

6 tablespoons canola or avocado oil, divided

¼ cup water

1 recipe Orange-Ginger Dipping Sauce (below), prepared

Toasted sesame seeds

TARA'S TIP

Wonton wrappers are readily available, but they are quite thin and delicate, so handle your dumplings gently at all stages to prevent them from tearing.

1. In a food processor, pulse mushrooms, ginger, and garlic until very finely chopped. Add slaw and pulse to chop. Add sesame oil, vinegar, orange juice, cilantro, and scallions. Pulse until mixture is evenly chopped and combined. Add sausage and pulse to just combine.

2. Working one at a time, place a level tablespoon of sausage mixture in the center of one wonton wrapper. Dip your finger in some water and wet the edges of the wrapper. Lift two opposite corners of the wrapper, and press together at the tip. Bring the remaining two corners together, overlapping like they are hugging the sausage packet. Press and pinch to seal together at the tip and edges. Place dumpling on a sheet of parchment. Repeat until all of the filling is used.

3. Heat 3 tablespoons oil in a large, high-sided nonstick skillet with a lid, over medium-high heat. Add dumplings in a single layer and reduce heat to medium. Cook until dumplings have a brown, crispy bottom, about 2 minutes. Add 2 tablespoons water and cover pan. Steam until dumplings are cooked through, 3 to 4 minutes. Remove cooked dumplings to a plate, and add remaining oil to skillet, repeat for remaining dumplings.

4. Serve with Orange-Ginger Dipping Sauce, sprinkled with sesame seeds if desired.

ORANGE-GINGER DIPPING SAUCE

⅓ cup low-sodium soy sauce

⅓ cup rice wine vinegar

3 tablespoons water

2 tablespoons light brown sugar

1 teaspoon sesame oil

¾ teaspoon orange zest

¾ teaspoon grated fresh ginger

1 teaspoon toasted sesame seeds

In a medium bowl, whisk together all ingredients. Serve immediately or store in refrigerator up to a week. Bring to room temperature and shake well before serving.

MAKES

4 SERVINGS

HANDS-ON TIME

35 MINUTES

TOTAL TIME

50 MINUTES

chicken in paper with carrot ribbons and golden raisins

WHO DOESN'T LOVE opening a personalized package? And when that package contains a wonderfully tender and flavorful mix of chicken and veggies, you'll want to serve presents at dinner more often. This fun French method of quick-cooking is called "en papillote," meaning "in paper," and produces a perfectly cooked meal in just a few minutes.

The parchment packet creates a little sauna for the chicken and allows the flavors of all the ingredients to infuse goodness into the chicken.

TARA'S TIP

Finding small chicken breasts is sometimes not easy, so simply cut two large breasts in half. The key is to pound the pieces to ½-inch thick so they cook quickly and evenly. Alternatively, you can slice the two large breasts in half, horizontally, creating two ½ inch-thick pieces.

4 small boneless, skinless chicken breasts (1¾ pounds total)

⅓ cup finely chopped flat-leaf parsley

1 clove garlic, minced

Zest of 1 lemon

1¼ teaspoons kosher salt, divided

¼ teaspoon red pepper flakes

1 teaspoon sumac

¼ teaspoon ground coriander

2 medium carrots, cut into ribbons with a vegetable peeler

1 tablespoon honey

4 slices lemon

⅓ cup golden raisins

¼ cup toasted pine nuts

1. Heat oven to 400°F. Put chicken breasts between 2 pieces of plastic wrap and use a meat mallet or the bottom of a pot to pound chicken to ½-inch thickness; set aside.

2. Prepare parchment packets: Cut 4 pieces of parchment measuring 12-by-16-inches. Fold each parchment rectangle in half crosswise to make an 8-by-12-inch rectangle. Cut out a large half-heart shape, making sure to leave the folded side uncut and using as much of the paper as you can. (You want the heart to be large.) Unfold each heart-shaped piece of parchment and set aside.

3. In a small bowl, combine parsley, garlic, lemon zest, ¾ teaspoon of the salt, red pepper flakes, sumac, and coriander. In a separate bowl, toss 1½ tablespoons of the parsley mixture, honey, and remaining ½ teaspoon salt with the carrots; set remaining parsley mixture aside.

4. Divide carrots between each piece of parchment, placing a small pile in the center of one half of the heart. (It should be right up against the fold mark but only on one half of the heart.) Sprinkle remaining parsley mixture over chicken breasts. Place chicken on top of the carrots, top with a lemon slice, some golden raisins, and 1 tablespoon pine nuts.

5. Fold parchment over the chicken to make a packet that looks like a half heart. Secure the edges by folding them together about every inch. Place all 4 packets on a baking sheet and bake 15 minutes.

6. Remove packets from oven and let rest 2 to 3 minutes. Snip just the tops of the packets with kitchen shears so that each person can fully tear open their own packet when ready to eat.

patsy's pepperoni-pizza pasta with ricotta

PATSY'S, the famous New York City pizzeria that perfected New York-style thin crust pizza, is just a few blocks from me on the Upper West Side. It's one of few remaining pizza shops that the city still allows to use a coal oven. Friends introduced me to my now-favorite topping combination at Patsy's: roasted sweet bell peppers, pepperoni, and creamy ricotta melted on top of a margarita-style pizza and cooked crisp in their coal ovens. I've never looked back.

If you can believe it, my NYC apartment doesn't have a coal oven (wink!), so recreating this pizza at home means getting creative. Instead of a crust, I use the next best Italian starch—pasta. The end result is really the best of Patsy's in a bowl. As a bonus, it's easy enough to make any night of the week.

MAKES

4 TO 6 SERVINGS

HANDS-ON TIME

25 MINUTES

TOTAL TIME

45 MINUTES

2 bell peppers, any color

1 (16-ounce) package orecchiette pasta

¾ cup sliced pepperoni

1 (24-ounce) jar marinara

½ teaspoon dried oregano

½ teaspoon dried parsley

½ teaspoon garlic powder

Pinch crushed red pepper flakes

1 cup whole milk ricotta

¼ cup finely grated Parmesan

Fresh basil

Crostini, broken into pieces (page 40)

1. Heat broiler to high with the rack 4 to 6 inches from the heating element. Place whole peppers on a foil-lined baking sheet and place under broiler. Roast until each side is charred, turning occasionally, 6 to 8 minutes. Cool, peel off skin, and cut into ½- to 1-inch strips; set aside.

2. Cook pasta in very salty water according to package directions, drain, and set aside.

3. In a small bowl, stir together ricotta and Parmesan and set aside.

4. In a large nonstick skillet over medium-high heat, sauté pepperoni slices until curled and cooked, 1 to 2 minutes. Remove from skillet and set aside. Reduce heat to medium-low and add marinara sauce to skillet with oregano, parsley, garlic powder, and red pepper flakes. Bring to a simmer over medium heat, then stir in orecchiette, peppers, and pepperoni.

5. To serve, portion pasta into bowls and top with a generous spoonful of ricotta, chopped basil, crostini crumbles, and extra Parmesan, if desired.

TARA'S TIP

To make the dish come together even more quickly, I often roast a bunch of bell peppers early in the week and keep them in the refrigerator to use later in pasta like this, on sandwiches, or in my morning eggs. To store, place roasted peppers in a glass jar, pour some olive oil over the top, cover, and refrigerate.

LOOKS DELICIOUS I use small, thick-cut pepperoni just like Patsy's. If you get the standard, thin-sliced version, cut the large pieces in half before cooking.

MAKES

4 SERVINGS

HANDS-ON TIME

35 MINUTES

TOTAL TIME

55 MINUTES

lemon–butter salmon with herbs and cucumber salad

I COULDN'T BE HAPPIER with the combo of butter, garlic, and lemon. These three ingredients are the most splendid seasoning for salmon. This salmon is sautéed in that combo with herbs, and that's all it needs to melt in your mouth.

I melt the butter with some olive oil to help prevent the butter from burning, then add the garlic and let it flavor the butter and oil before cooking the fish. I add loads of fresh herbs to make sure this will be the perfect meal. The crisp, acidic cucumber salad cuts the richness of the salmon and is the ideal companion in every way.

TARA'S TIP

To save time, ask the fishmonger to skin your salmon so you don't have to do it at home. Or, if you want, you can keep the skin on. It's just not necessary for this dish, as it doesn't add any extra flavor.

2 lemons

¾ of a 12-inch English cucumber

1 cup grape tomatoes, sliced in half

¼ cup finely diced red onion

Kosher salt, to taste

Pepper, to taste

3 tablespoons extra-virgin olive oil, divided

¼ cup minced herbs, such as parsley and chives, divided

4 tablespoons unsalted butter

1 clove garlic, minced

4 (4-ounce) skinless salmon filets

1. Make the salad and dressing: Slice cucumber into thin slices and toss with tomatoes and red onion in a medium bowl. In a separate small bowl, juice one lemon and mix with ¼ teaspoon kosher salt. Whisk in 2 tablespoons of the olive oil and 1 tablespoon of the minced herbs. Pour dressing over cucumber-tomato mixture and toss to coat; set aside.

2. Make the salmon: Slice remaining lemon into thin slices and set aside.

3. Melt butter in a large, nonstick skillet over medium-high heat with remaining 1 tablespoon olive oil and garlic. When butter is melted, season salmon filets with salt and pepper and add to the hot butter. Sauté until the bottom is golden brown, 3 to 4 minutes. Turn filets over and cook another 1 to 2 minutes, until salmon is just cooked through, or cooked to your desired doneness. Medium-rare salmon should reach 125°F on an instant-read thermometer inserted in thickest part of the filet. Transfer salmon to a serving platter.

4. Add lemon slices and remaining 3 tablespoons herbs to the skillet and let cook about 1 minute. Remove pan from heat.

5. Serve lemons and herb butter atop salmon with cucumber salad on the side. If desired, garnish salad and salmon with extra herbs.

moroccan squash soup with crispy spiced chickpeas

MAKES

8 TO 10 SERVINGS

HANDS-ON TIME

25 MINUTES

TOTAL TIME

50 MINUTES

THE HONEY-ROASTED, spice-coated, crispy chickpeas really make this recipe unique. Sure, the velvety, perfectly seasoned, sweet-and-savory soup is special, too, but back to those chickpeas!

This recipe yields a lot! It's so easy to put together, I like to make enough to freeze some for later. My next cozy meal is only a thaw away, which gives me time to make some extra chickpeas.

⅛ teaspoon ground cloves

⅛ teaspoon ground allspice

⅛ teaspoon cayenne

½ teaspoon ground cinnamon

½ teaspoon ground coriander

¾ teaspoon ground cumin

¾ teaspoon ground ginger

½ teaspoon kosher salt

⅛ teaspoon ground black pepper

2 (15-ounce) cans chickpeas, drained, divided

2 tablespoons honey

4 tablespoons olive oil, divided

2 medium onions, chopped (4 cups)

8 cups peeled and chopped butternut squash (2½ pounds)

3 (15-ounce) cans low-sodium chicken or vegetable broth

Chopped flat-leaf parsley, for garnish

Toasted sesame seeds, for garnish

1. In a small bowl, combine the cloves, allspice, cayenne, cinnamon, coriander, cumin, ginger, salt, and pepper; set aside.

2. Heat oven to 400°F. Set aside ½ cup of the chickpeas for the soup. Pat remaining chickpeas dry with a paper towel. In a medium bowl, toss dried chickpeas with ½ teaspoon of the spice mixture, the honey, and 2 tablespoons olive oil. Spread the chickpeas on a parchment-lined, rimmed baking sheet and roast until crisp, stirring once halfway through, about 25 minutes total.

3. Meanwhile, heat 2 tablespoons oil over medium-high heat in a 6-quart pot. Add onions and sauté until translucent, 4 to 5 minutes. Add squash, reserved ½ cup chickpeas, and remaining spice mixture. Cook another 5 minutes, stirring occasionally.

4. Add broth and bring to a simmer. Reduce heat to medium-low, cover and cook until squash is tender, about 20 minutes.

5. Transfer soup to a blender in two batches and blend until very smooth. Return to the pot to keep warm unless serving immediately. Serve soup topped with the honey-spiced chickpeas, some parsley, and sesame seeds.

sweet glazed sausage tartine with greens

MAKES

4 SERVINGS

HANDS-ON TIME

20 MINUTES

TOTAL TIME

20 MINUTES

TARTINE is the fantastic French word for open-faced sandwich. Using a French name seems to fancy up a sandwich just enough to feel luxurious while loading your toast with all sorts of goodness and eating it with a knife and fork. Of course, you can also use your hands; it is a sandwich, after all! A hearty green like escarole or frisée holds up best to the glazed sausage, creating the ultimate one-slice-not-two sandwich. Move over avocado toast!

4 links sweet Italian sausage

1 recipe Savory-Sweet Apricot Glaze (page 172), prepared

4 large slices rustic bread

Extra-virgin olive oil

1 recipe Parmesan Herb White Bean Dip (page 21), prepared

2 cups escarole, frisée, or similar greens

1. Heat grill to medium and grill the sausages, turning occasionally, until cooked through, 8 to 10 minutes. Sausage should register 160°F. on an instant-read thermometer.

2. Slice sausage into pieces, and brush liberally with Savory-Sweet Apricot Glaze.

3. Brush rustic bread slices with olive oil and grill until toasted and marked on both sides.

4. Cover toast liberally with Parmesan Herb White Bean Dip. Top with sliced, glazed sausage and a few greens. Drizzle with some of the remaining apricot glaze.

> **TARA'S TIP**
>
> I used fresh thyme instead of rosemary in my apricot glaze for this recipe. It goes so well with the white bean dip, and you can add extra for garnish if you'd like.
>
> You can skip the grill and cook the sausage and toasts under a hot broiler.

MAKES

4 TO 6
SERVINGS

HANDS-ON TIME

30 MINUTES

TOTAL TIME

30 MINUTES

street tacos with spiced chicken and pepper jack

I REFER TO THESE as "Mary's Favorite Tacos" because they are made on a regular basis at my mom's house. I think there are two things that make my version her fave. The first is the chicken rub. Mom makes it by the cupful and stores it in the pantry. The spice combo is perfect on a quick-grilled piece of chicken. The second is melting the Pepper Jack cheese on the tortillas before assembling the tacos. It's pretty heavenly and Mexican-food-loving-mom approved.

Since authentic street tacos have only a few staple toppings, maybe some hot sauce, and some really flavorful meat, it's easy to make this taco-stand-favorite at home.

3 boneless, skinless chicken breasts (1½ to 2 pounds)	2 tablespoons olive oil
1 teaspoon ground cumin	8 ounces grated Pepper Jack cheese (2 cups)
1 teaspoon garlic powder	White onion, diced
1 teaspoon chili powder	Chopped cilantro
1 teaspoon kosher salt	Lime wedges
12 corn tortillas	Hot sauce

1. Heat oven to 350°F and center the two oven racks. Line 2 baking sheets with foil.

2. Place chicken breasts between 2 pieces of plastic wrap and pound to just under 1-inch thick with a meat mallet or heavy pot. Alternatively, cut breasts in half, horizontally, to make thinner pieces.

3. Heat grill to medium-high. In a small bowl, combine cumin, garlic powder, chili powder, and salt; rub spice mixture all over chicken. Grill chicken, turning once, until just cooked through, 8 to 10 minutes total. Let rest before slicing, as described in step 5.

4. Brush tortillas with oil and lay flat on the baking sheets. Bake until warm, 5 to 7 minutes. Top each tortilla with a few tablespoons of cheese. Return to oven until cheese is melted.

5. Slice hot chicken and add to tortillas. Top with onion and cilantro. Serve with a squeeze of lime juice and hot sauce.

LOOKS DELICIOUS I toast my corn tortillas over the grill flame or my gas stove burner before brushing them with oil. This gives them a toasty flavor and pretty look.

spicy pork cutlets with corn and avocado salad

MAKES

4 TO 6 SERVINGS

HANDS-ON TIME

30 MINUTES

TOTAL TIME

40 MINUTES

I'VE SEASONED these cutlets with Southwest flavors, making them "milanesa," the Mexican word for breaded and fried meat. In Austria and Germany, you would call this "schnitzel," in Japan it's "tonkatsu," and in France it's "escalope." Whatever the language, these crispy, golden cutlets that are breaded and sizzled to perfection are worth their weight in gold. Add my creamy, tangy, and slightly spicy chipotle yogurt dressing and you've just traveled to the end of the food-heaven rainbow.

DRESSING

¾ cup plain whole-milk yogurt

1 tablespoon white wine vinegar

2 teaspoons sugar

1 tablespoon lime juice

3 tablespoons water

1 chipotle chili from a 7-ounce can chipotle in adobo, seeds discarded

2 teaspoons adobo sauce from canned chipotle in adobo

⅛ teaspoon kosher salt, to taste

⅓ cup extra-virgin olive oil or avocado oil

CUTLETS

1 (1¼-pound) pork tenderloin, silver skin removed

1 cup plain bread crumbs

1 teaspoon chili powder

1 large egg

1 tablespoon lime juice

4 tablespoons canola or avocado oil, divided

SALAD

2 ears corn, husked and charred

1 (5-ounce) bag mixed baby greens

⅓ cup chopped chives

1 ripe avocado, diced

Lime wedges, for garnish

1. Make dressing: Combine yogurt, vinegar, lime juice, water, the chipotle chili, adobo sauce, and kosher salt in a blender; blend until smooth. With blender running, add olive oil in a slow stream, blending until thickened and emulsified. Season to taste with salt and set aside.

2. Make cutlets: Cut tenderloin into eight pieces crosswise. Place each piece between 2 sheets of plastic wrap and pound gently with a meat mallet or heavy pot to ¼-inch thickness. Lightly sprinkle cutlets with salt. Place on a baking sheet and set aside.

3. Combine bread crumbs and chili powder in a wide, shallow dish or pie pan. Whisk together egg and lime juice in a shallow bowl. Dip cutlets, 1 at a time, in egg mixture (allowing excess to drip back into bowl), then in bread crumbs, turning to coat well. Transfer back to baking sheet.

4. Heat 2 tablespoons oil in a large nonstick skillet over medium-high heat until hot but not smoking. Add half of the cutlets and cook, turning once, until golden brown and cooked through, 3 to 4 minutes total. Transfer cooked cutlets

TARA'S TIP

Charring corn is quick and easy: Heat a little bit of oil in a cast-iron skillet and add two ears of corn, cooking until charred on all sides. You can also give them a quick turn on a hot grill. Let cool and cut the corn off the cobs. Or use frozen, thawed corn and broil it for 2 minutes on a baking sheet.

Try swapping pork for either chicken or turkey cutlets. Just make sure to slice or pound them to about ¼-inch thickness so they cook quickly.

to a serving platter and wipe out pan with a paper towel. Add remaining 2 table-spoons oil to the skillet and cook remaining cutlets as described above.

5. Make salad: Cut kernels from corn and add to a large bowl. Gently toss with salad greens, avocado, and chives. Serve salad alongside cutlets, with dressing drizzled over both and lime wedges for squeezing.

THAI PEANUT SAUCE

WHEN I EAT chicken satay at my favorite Thai restaurant, I could just drink that peanut sauce! I love it so much. It's not inherently Thai, but it does have a lot of flavors found in authentic Thai food. This sauce is fantastic with chicken or beef satay, but it can also be thinned out with a little water or extra vinegar for a salad dressing. I'll even drizzle it on a grilled chicken sandwich!

MAKES

1¼ CUPS SAUCE

HANDS-ON TIME

10 MINUTES

TOTAL TIME

20 MINUTES

1 cup full-fat, unsweetened coconut milk

1½ tablespoons Thai red or Massaman curry paste

⅓ cup natural (unsweetened) creamy peanut butter

½ teaspoon kosher salt

⅓ cup light brown sugar

1 tablespoon apple cider vinegar

1 teaspoon fish sauce

¼ cup water

Small pinch red pepper flakes

1. In a medium saucepan over medium heat, bring coconut milk, curry paste, peanut butter, salt, sugar, vinegar, fish sauce, water, and pepper flakes to a simmer, whisking constantly.

2. Reduce heat to low and simmer 3 to 4 minutes, being careful not to let the mixture scorch the bottom of the pan. Remove pan from heat, let the sauce cool to room temperature, and serve.

3. Sauce can be refrigerated in an airtight container for up to 5 days.

MAKES

6 SERVINGS

HANDS-ON TIME

35 MINUTES

TOTAL TIME

45 MINUTES

peanut noodle and pork "satay"

I TURNED my favorite satay appetizer into a no-fuss, no-skewer weeknight dinner. Traditional Thai satay is made with pork cutlets, but we are used to the American standard of little chicken pieces marinated in exotic spices, ginger, and fish sauce and grilled on little bamboo skewers.

Here, you'll mix some of those same great flavors into ground pork and skip the skewers. Serve the deliciousness over rice noodles with my Thai Peanut Sauce.

TARA'S TIP

Rice noodles can be tricky if you aren't familiar with them. The key is to not overcook them or they will turn mushy. Test them along the way and drain them as soon as they are tender.

1 (14-ounce) package rice noodles

1 recipe Thai Peanut Sauce (page 143), prepared

2 tablespoons olive oil

¼ Napa cabbage, cut into wedges or large squares (about 3 cups)

1 pound ground pork

3 cloves garlic, minced

2 teaspoons light brown sugar

¾ teaspoon turmeric

1 teaspoon ground coriander

½ teaspoon fish sauce

1 tablespoon low-sodium soy sauce

½ cup chopped basil

½ cup chopped mint

2 Persian cucumbers, cut into ½-inch pieces

Crushed peanuts

Lime wedges

1. Cook rice noodles according to package directions. Drain and toss with ½ cup Thai Peanut Sauce in a large bowl.

2. Heat oil over medium-high heat in a large skillet. Add cabbage and cook just until bright green and tender, 2 to 3 minutes. Remove cabbage from skillet and set aside.

3. Add pork and garlic to the same hot skillet. Cook, breaking pork into very small pieces, until almost cooked through, about 3 minutes. Add brown sugar, turmeric, coriander, fish sauce, and soy sauce. Cook another 2 minutes. Remove from heat and add cabbage back to pan; set aside.

4. Serve noodles topped with pork and cabbage; top with cucumbers, basil, mint, and crushed peanuts, to taste. Drizzle as generously as desired with extra peanut sauce, and a squeeze of lime.

MEALS FOR GATHERING

moroccan kebabs with chermoula sauce

THIS IS YOUR new party-table centerpiece. Colorful and tasty skewers arranged around a dipping sauce is easy to make happen and creates a stunning platter. And the chermoula sauce (pronounced like the singer "Cher" then "moola," like money) is expressive and lemony. The sauce is based on a Moroccan and Tunisian relish with a strong herb and spice situation. I keep the skewers of meat and veggies small so they can be bite-sized for a gathering, but you can make them more robust if you'd like to serve this recipe as a meal.

MAKES

15 TO 20 SERVINGS,
ABOUT 45 SKEWERS

HANDS-ON TIME

1 HOUR 30 MINUTES

TOTAL TIME

2 HOURS

½ teaspoon turmeric

½ teaspoon ground black pepper

¼ cup warm water

4 tablespoons extra-virgin olive oil, divided

3 tablespoons fresh lemon juice

1 tablespoon tomato paste

5 cloves garlic, chopped

3 teaspoons kosher salt, divided

2 teaspoons smoked paprika

2 teaspoons ground cumin

1 tablespoon ground coriander

¼ teaspoon ground cinnamon

2½ pounds boneless, skinless chicken thighs, cut into strips that are 2 inches long and ½ inch thick

2 yellow or orange bell peppers, cut into 1-inch squares

2 small zucchini, thinly sliced into strips with a vegetable peeler

1 (14.4-ounce) bag frozen pearl onions, thawed

1 pint grape or cherry tomatoes

45 (6-inch) bamboo skewers, soaked in water 20 minutes

1 recipe Chermoula Sauce (page 161), prepared

> **TARA'S TIP**
>
> Alternatively, you can broil the skewers in batches on high, until cooked through, 12 to 14 minutes for the chicken, turning once.
>
> Pearl onions are a pretty alternative to chopped or sliced onions. I also like to use thin strips of zucchini folded like ribbon instead of a large piece. This helps the kebabs cook quickly, so there is not a lot of tending.

1. In a large bowl, whisk together turmeric and pepper with ¼ cup warm water. Let sit 3 minutes. Whisk in 2 tablespoons of the olive oil, the lemon juice, tomato paste, garlic, 1 teaspoon salt, paprika, cumin, coriander, and cinnamon.

2. Season chicken strips with 1 teaspoon salt and add to the marinade. Cover and refrigerate to marinate 30 minutes.

3. In a large bowl, toss peppers, zucchini, onions, and tomatoes with remaining 2 tablespoons olive oil and season with 1 teaspoon kosher salt. Thread chicken on half of the skewers and vegetables on the other half, adding several slices of zucchini to each skewer. Discard chicken marinade.

4. Heat grill to medium-high. Grill skewers, turning occasionally, until chicken is cooked through, 10 to 12 minutes total. Remove the vegetables from the grill as soon as they are done; they will cook faster than the chicken.

5. Serve on a platter with the chermoula sauce for drizzling and dipping.

LOOKS DELICIOUS Arranging these colorful and tasty skewers around their dipping sauce is an easy way to create a stunning platter.

MAKES

10 TO 12 SERVINGS

HANDS-ON TIME

25 MINUTES

TOTAL TIME

2 HOURS

golden roast chickens with pan sauce

THE SMELL OF CHICKEN roasting is one of the most comforting and delicious things on earth! When I need to feed a crowd, this is my go-to recipe. It's just as easy to roast two chickens as one, with no extra work. For guests or nice dinners, I serve the chicken with a pan sauce and a few great sides. Other times, I roast two chickens to shred some meat to use for meals later in the week or month.

On a leisurely weekend, or if a crowd is coming over, take a few minutes to get these two chickens in your oven. These birds are seasoned with a special mixture of coriander, garlic, and lemon, making a pan sauce that's divine.

2 (4½- to 5-pound) whole chickens, giblets removed

2½ teaspoons kosher salt, divided

3 yellow onions, peeled and cut into large wedges

1 lemon, sliced

3 ribs celery, cut into 2-inch pieces

2 small bunches of herbs, such as thyme, oregano, or sage

3 tablespoons unsalted butter, softened

1 clove garlic, minced

2 teaspoons ground coriander

1 (14.5-ounce) can low-sodium chicken broth, for pan sauce (see variation below)

1. Heat oven to 400°F and adjust rack to the lower third of oven. Sprinkle the inside of each chicken with ¼ teaspoon salt, then fill each with ⅓ of the onion wedges, lemon wedges, and celery pieces. Put 1 bunch herbs in each chicken. Place remaining ⅓ vegetables and lemon slices in the bottom of a roasting pan. Tie chicken legs together with kitchen string, then place both chickens on top of vegetables in pan and pat skin dry with paper towels.

2. In a small bowl, mix together butter, garlic, and coriander. Rub each chicken with mixture and sprinkle with remaining salt.

3. Roast chickens until golden brown and juices run clear, about 1 hour 20 minutes, tenting with foil if parts become too brown. An instant-read thermometer inserted under a thigh should read 170°F. (Dark meat may be slightly pink.) Remove from oven and let rest 10 minutes.

4. Slice and serve hot with pan sauce (see variation below) or shred to use in other recipes. Wrap leftovers and store in refrigerator up to 3 days.

ROAST CHICKEN WITH PAN SAUCE VARIATION: After step 3 above, remove vegetables from roasting pan and transfer juices and any browned bits to a medium saucepan. Place over medium-high heat, add broth, and bring to a boil. Simmer until liquid has reduced by half, about 10 minutes. Strain sauce through a sieve into a serving dish and serve alongside chicken.

savory romesco and almond tart

ROMESCO is a flavorful Spanish sauce with tomatoes and dried, sweet red peppers at its base and enhanced with nuts and garlic. The recipes for this classic sauce have morphed and changed over generations, and most often you will find romesco made from roasted red peppers and only a little tomato, if any. My favorite romesco is this zesty version with plenty of almonds and a splash of vinegar and paprika. It's delicious as a dip or condiment, served with fish or veggies, or spread on toast.

Paired with the buttery pastry crust and greens, this tart is sophisticated, unique, and extremely delicious. The olive oil helps the filling hold its shape when the tart is chilled. I also love the salad combo of date, almond, and cheese and often serve it on its own.

MAKES

1 (9-INCH) TART
6 TO 8 SERVINGS

HANDS-ON TIME

30 MINUTES

TOTAL TIME

2 HOURS 30 MINUTES

½ recipe All-Butter Double-Crust Pastry (page 198)

ROMESCO

¾ cup roasted and salted almonds

1 clove garlic

¾ teaspoon kosher salt

1 teaspoon red wine vinegar

1 teaspoon sweet paprika

¼ cup extra-virgin olive oil

1 (12-ounce) jar roasted red bell peppers, drained

SALAD

4 cups mixed greens, such as frisée, red leaf, and flat-leaf parsley

5 dates, pitted and thinly sliced

¼ cup roasted and salted almonds, crushed

½ cup Manchego cheese, shaved with vegetable peeler

2 tablespoons extra-virgin olive oil

1½ tablespoons fresh lemon juice

TARA'S TIP

Hazelnuts are often used instead of almonds in romesco. Feel free to swap them in this recipe for a truly decadent flavor.

Use smoked paprika in place of sweet in the sauce and pair it with my roasted veggies in the Roasted Cauliflower and Smoky Romesco recipe (page 69).

1. Heat oven to 400°F. On a lightly floured surface, roll the pastry dough into an 11-inch circle, transfer to an 8- or 9-inch tart pan with removable bottom and gently fit into pan and up the sides. Trim excess dough flush with the top of the pan. Prick bottom of crust all over with a fork. Blind-bake the pastry following the instructions for blind baking on the All-Butter Double-Crust Pastry recipe.

2. For the romesco: In a food processor, purée the almonds, garlic, salt, vinegar, paprika, and olive oil until very smooth. Add red peppers and purée.

3. Spread filling into cooled crust in an even layer and chill tart at least 1 hour or up to 4 hours.

4. For the salad: In a medium bowl, toss together the greens, dates, crushed almonds, and shaved Manchego with olive oil, lemon juice, and season with salt and pepper to taste. Garnish tart with some of the salad then serve each piece with extra greens.

MAKES

12 TO 14 SERVINGS

HANDS-ON TIME

40 MINUTES

TOTAL TIME

40 MINUTES

the never-ending party sub

THIS IS MY KIND of sandwich! It's deceptively easy to make this impressive, three-foot party sub. Trim the ends off two loaves of grocery store French bread or ciabatta and match them together. What really brings the grandeur is the filling. All that roast beef, ham, and turkey slathered with a bacon mayo and topped with a lightly pickled, thin-sliced zucchini and shallot combo plus some ultra-creamy Havarti cheese. It's official: you are the party queen.

3 small zucchini	1 cup mayonnaise
1 tablespoon granulated sugar	8 slices cooked bacon, finely chopped
¾ teaspoon kosher salt	1 pound sliced turkey
1 small shallot, thinly sliced root to tip	1 pound sliced roast beef
2 tablespoons chopped dill	1 pound sliced deli ham
1 tablespoon white wine vinegar	3 tomatoes, thinly sliced
2 large bakery loaves French or ciabatta bread	12 ounces Havarti cheese, sliced

1. Using a mandolin or a vegetable peeler, thinly slice the zucchini lengthwise into long strips. In a medium bowl, toss zucchini strips with sugar, salt, shallot, dill, and vinegar. Set aside, but stir occasionally.

2. Slice French bread loaves in half horizontally. Trim one end from each loaf and match the cut ends to create one large sandwich. Line up several cutting boards (or use one long, 4-foot board) on the table and place bottom half of loaves on top to assemble.

3. In a small bowl, stir together the mayonnaise and bacon and spread evenly on the bottom half of the connected loaves. Top with the sliced turkey, roast beef, ham, tomatoes, and cheese.

4. Drain liquid from zucchini mixture and add to the sandwich. Cover with the bread tops.

TARA'S TIP

This three-footer will not fit in your fridge! Assembling the sandwich only takes 10 to 15 minutes and it can sit at room temperature for up to 3 hours, so make it just before serving. Wrap leftovers and store in the fridge.

LOOKS DELICIOUS You can line up several cutting boards on your table to serve this beauty, or make your own 4-foot wooden plank like I did. A standard, 1-by-4-board, sanded and cleaned, is all you need. Simply rub the plank with mineral oil or use a food-safe white wash on it.

OVEN-ROASTED PLUM TOMATOES

THESE JUICY, concentrated tomatoes are easy to make—they just take some time in the oven to roast and caramelize. If it's summertime, you can roast them on foil, in a covered, low-heat grill. I use them on sandwiches, grilled bread, snack boards, in pasta, and in salads.

18 plum tomatoes, stems removed and sliced in half lengthwise

¼ cup olive oil

1 teaspoon kosher salt

½ teaspoon ground black pepper

1 tablespoon dried oregano

1. Heat oven to 375°F. Remove and discard seeds and pulp from tomatoes, and in a medium bowl, gently toss the tomatoes with the olive oil, salt, pepper, and oregano to coat. Arrange tomatoes on a foil-lined rimmed baking sheet, cut sides up.

2. Roast 30 minutes. Reduce oven temperature to 300°F. Roast an additional 90 minutes until tomatoes are just starting to caramelize. Turn tomatoes skin-side up and roast an additional 10 minutes.

3. Let tomatoes cool on a wire rack and then remove from pan. Tomatoes can be stored in an airtight container in the refrigerator up to a week.

MAKES

3 CUPS

HANDS-ON TIME

35 MINUTES

TOTAL TIME
2 HOURS
35 MINUTES

MEALS FOR GATHERING

sublime sausage pesto lasagna

IN THE SUMMER, when fresh basil is plentiful, I make loads of my Classic Pesto and freeze it in small quantities so I can enjoy a little anytime. That practice inspired this pesto lasagna recipe. I was preparing for a photo shoot one day and needed freezer space, so the pesto and Italian sausage in the back of the freezer had to go! I mixed extra pesto into the ricotta layer, and this glorious variation on classic lasagna was born.

A regular 9-by-13-inch baking dish won't be able to hold all 4 generous layers of goodness between the noodles, so make sure to use a deep-dish lasagna pan.

MAKES

9 TO 12 SERVINGS

HANDS-ON TIME

50 MINUTES

TOTAL TIME

1 HOUR 45 MINUTES

1 pound spicy or sweet Italian sausage links, casings removed

1 pound lean ground beef

1½ teaspoons kosher salt, divided

2 cloves garlic, minced

¾ teaspoon fennel seeds, crushed

1 medium yellow onion, finely diced

2 (24-ounce) jars marinara sauce

2 cups whole milk ricotta

1 cup Classic Pesto (page 160)

¼ cup shredded Parmesan

1 (16-ounce) package lasagna noodles

1 pound mozzarella, grated (4 cups)

> **TARA'S TIP**
>
> I love traditional lasagna noodles for this dish because they are sturdy and have those classic curled edges. If you'd prefer, you can use fresh pasta sheets instead.

1. In a large, high-sided skillet, sauté pan, or Dutch oven, over medium-high heat, combine the sausage, ground beef, 1 teaspoon salt, garlic, fennel seeds, and onion. Cook, breaking up meat into very small pieces, until meat is cooked through, about 10 minutes. Remove from heat and add the marinara sauce. Stir to combine and set aside.

2. Heat oven to 375°F. Cook lasagna noodles in very salty water according to package directions, drain, and lay flat on a plate.

3. Meanwhile, in a medium bowl, stir together the ricotta, pesto, remaining ½ teaspoon salt, and Parmesan.

4. To assemble lasagna, spread ¾ cup of the meat sauce in the bottom of a large lasagna pan. Add a single layer of noodles. Spread ⅓ of the ricotta mixture on the noodles and top with 1 cup of the shredded mozzarella. Repeat by adding a layer (this time about 2 cups) of meat sauce, more noodles, another ⅓ of the ricotta, and another cup of the mozzarella. Repeat this process one more time, and then layer on remaining noodles and meat sauce, in that order. You will have 1 cup mozzarella left; set that aside to use at the end of the cooking time.

5. Cover pan with foil and bake, until heated through and cheese is melted, about 45 minutes. Uncover and sprinkle with remaining 1 cup mozzarella. Bake until the cheese is melted, about 10 more minutes. Alternatively, broil a few minutes to melt the cheese and get a golden top.

6. Remove lasagna and let rest 10 to 20 minutes before slicing and serving.

LOOKS DELICIOUS Lasagna is inherently messy to serve! It takes a lot of time and a few tricks to food style a perfect block of lasagna on a plate for a photo. The resting time after it comes out of the oven is key to slicing up fairly stable pieces. Letting the lasagna rest allows the noodles to absorb extra juices and the cheese to set up just a bit.

CLASSIC PESTO

MAKES

2 CUPS

HANDS-ON TIME

15 MINUTES

TOTAL TIME

15 MINUTES

THIS SAVORY herb sauce is super easy to whip up. And classic pesto isn't just for pasta. Whisk it into a balsamic dressing, top grilled shrimp with it, or add a dollop to your scrambled eggs.

¾ cup lightly toasted pine nuts	2 cloves garlic, roughly chopped
4 cups packed basil leaves	½ teaspoon kosher salt
1 cup finely grated Parmesan	¾ cup extra-virgin olive oil

1. To toast pine nuts, bake them in a 350°F oven until fragrant, 5 to 6 minutes.

2. Combine basil, Parmesan, pine nuts, garlic, and salt in the bowl of a food processor. Pulse until mixture is finely chopped. With the motor running, slowly pour the oil into the feed tube. Process until well combined.

3. Use immediately or store in the refrigerator up to a week. Pesto can also be frozen in airtight container up to a month.

TARA'S TIP

In winter months when basil isn't as plentiful, use 1 cup basil and a mix of 3 cups flat-leaf parsley and arugula.

SWEET AND SAVORY CRANBERRY CHUTNEY

MAKES

1½ CUPS

HANDS-ON TIME

30 MINUTES

TOTAL TIME

30 MINUTES

I KEEP CRANBERRIES in the freezer and on hand all year long to make this chutney, and I often use it as a sandwich spread or over chicken or salmon. I recommend trying it on roasted sweet potatoes or atop ricotta toasts.

For Thanksgiving and other times when a more autumnal flavor is welcome, swap the lemon zest and pomegranate juice for orange zest and orange juice. Add a teaspoon of grated fresh ginger as well.

1 tablespoon olive oil	⅔ cup granulated sugar
1 shallot, finely chopped (about ⅓ cup)	⅓ cup pomegranate or cranberry juice
1 (12-ounce) bag fresh or frozen cranberries	½ teaspoon kosher salt
	Pinch ground black pepper

1. Heat oil in a 2-quart saucepan over medium heat. Sauté shallot until just softened, 2 to 3 minutes.

2. Stir in cranberries, sugar, juice, salt, and pepper. Bring to a simmer and cook until berries just begin to burst and sauce is thickening, 8 to 10 minutes.

3. Remove from heat and let cool. Serve warm or chilled. Refrigerate chutney in an airtight container up to a week.

CHERMOULA SAUCE

THIS SPICED herb sauce is used on fish, meat, chicken, and vegetables. A heady and unique flavor that's great with the Moroccan Kebabs Platter (page 149).

MAKES

⅔ CUP SAUCE

HANDS-ON TIME

15 MINUTES

TOTAL TIME

15 MINUTES

½ teaspoon coriander seeds	1 teaspoon smoked paprika
½ teaspoon cumin seeds	¾ teaspoon kosher salt
2 cloves garlic	Pinch red pepper flakes
¼ cup extra-virgin olive oil	1 cup packed cilantro
¼ teaspoon lemon zest	1 cup packed flat-leaf parsley
2 tablespoons fresh lemon juice	½ cup packed mint leaves

1. In a small skillet over medium-high heat, toast coriander and cumin seeds until fragrant, 1 to 2 minutes. Remove from heat and crush in a mortar and pestle or with the bottom of a pan.

2. In the bowl of a food processor, combine crushed seeds, garlic, olive oil, lemon zest, lemon juice, paprika, salt, and red pepper flakes. Pulse to finely chop garlic. Add cilantro, parsley, and mint and blend until herbs are well combined. Store sauce in refrigerator until ready to use, up to 3 days.

HANDS-ON TIME

15 MINUTES

TOTAL TIME

3 HOURS
10 MINUTES

TARA'S TIP

For a complete meal, serve these with Garlic and Sumac Roasted Broccoli (page 73) or Watermelon Arugula Salad (page 54).

sticky spiced drumsticks

KIDS OF ALL AGES love a drumstick, and this sweet-sticky version is a hit. This is a tasty, easy dinner you can put together in the morning and bake at dinnertime. Since I'm not frying these little chicken legs, I like to go skinless. Ask your butcher to skin the drumsticks, or take a few extra minutes and do it yourself. Don plastic gloves and use kitchen shears to cut the skin. A paper towel allows you the best grip to tear off the skin.

¾ cup chili sauce (such as Heinz)

3 tablespoons low-sodium soy sauce

1 tablespoon grated ginger

½ teaspoon red pepper flakes

4 cloves garlic, minced

¼ cup apple cider or apple juice

2 tablespoons light brown sugar

12 skinless chicken drumsticks

2 teaspoons toasted sesame seeds

3 scallions, white and green parts sliced

1. In a medium bowl, whisk together chili sauce, soy sauce, ginger, red pepper flakes, garlic, apple cider, and brown sugar. Place drumsticks in a large bowl or large zip-top bag and pour sauce over top. Cover bowl, or seal bag, and refrigerate at least 2 hours.

2. Heat oven to 400°F. Place chicken and marinade in a foil-lined rimmed baking sheet. Roast 40 minutes, turning chicken halfway through. Set broiler to high and move chicken under broiler for 2 minutes, until sauce has caramelized.

3. Serve, brushed with remaining sauce from pan and sprinkled with sesame seeds and scallions.

LOOKS DELICIOUS Curled shreds of scallions are unexpected and playful. Cut your scallions into 2- to 3-inch lengths and then, using a sharp paring knife, thinly slice the lengths. They'll curl on their own as they wait to be used as a garnish.

french bistro mushroom burgers with brie and onions

THE SLIGHTLY caramelized, Worcestershire-glistening onions are a special touch on these delicious burgers. I love how the Brie melts on top of the burger, creating an almost saucelike cream. Earthy mushrooms hidden in the beef add a nutty, buttery, complex flavor with a meaty texture. I chop the mushrooms small so they easily melt into the burger. I think your cook-out crowd will be extremely happy with every bite of this twist on the iconic burger.

MAKES

4 SERVINGS

HANDS-ON TIME

25 MINUTES

TOTAL TIME

1 HOUR 5 MINUTES

3 small yellow onions, peeled and cut into ¼-inch onion rings

3 tablespoons Worcestershire sauce, divided

3 tablespoons olive oil, divided

6 ounces cremini or baby bella mushrooms, cleaned

2 tablespoons unsalted butter

2 teaspoons chopped thyme

1 clove garlic, minced

1 pound ground beef

1 teaspoon kosher salt

¼ teaspoon ground black pepper

Mayonnaise or garlic aioli

1 wedge Brie or triple cream cheese such as Saint-André

Baby arugula, for topping

4 brioche or hamburger buns

TARA'S TIP

Ground mushrooms in burgers is part of a sustainability movement to help extend ground beef so less is used. The mushrooms also impart a delicious umami flavor.

You can make your own garlic aioli in a blender. Combine 1 head of roasted garlic, squeezed from the skins, 2 teaspoons lemon juice, and 1¼ cups mayonnaise. Blend until smooth.

1. Heat oven to 400°F. Line a rimmed baking sheet with foil. Spread onion rings on pan and toss with 2 tablespoons Worcestershire sauce and 2 tablespoons olive oil. Cover loosely with foil and roast until soft, 8 to 10 minutes. Uncover and roast until caramelized, 12 to 15 minutes more. Set aside.

2. In a food processor, chop mushrooms until the largest pieces are the size of peas; set aside. Heat butter, 1 tablespoon olive oil, thyme, and garlic in a medium skillet over medium heat. Add mushrooms and sauté, stirring often, until just soft and mushroom juices are cooked away, 5 to 6 minutes. Remove from heat and let cool slightly.

3. In a large bowl, use your hands to combine mushroom mixture, ground beef, remaining 1 tablespoon Worcestershire sauce, salt, and pepper; mixture will be wet. Shape mixture into 4 patties, ¾-inches thick.

4. Broil, pan fry, or grill patties until cooked to medium-well doneness (155°F on an instant-read thermometer), about 4 minutes per side.

5. Assemble burgers on buns with aioli, arugula, thick slices of Brie, and onion rings.

LOOKS DELICIOUS This recipe makes large bistro-style burgers, so feel free to divide the meat mixture into 6 patties to make more servings.

MAKES

9 TO 11 CUPS
SHREDDED
CARNITAS

HANDS-ON TIME

30 MINUTES

TOTAL TIME

7 HOURS
30 MINUTES

cuban garlic–lime carnitas with mojo

MOJO IS THAT magical charisma that charms the socks off people. And in traditional Cuban cooking, it is any sauce made with garlic, olive oil, and citrus. I'd like to think my carnitas recipe covers both mojo areas! The marinating is essential to get the perfect flavor, and the lime and garlic mellow exquisitely as this roast slow cooks.

Leftovers can be reheated in the mojo juices and offer endless options for weeknight dinners. Serve with my Grilled-Pineapple Coconut Rice (page 86), in tacos, on my Jalapeño Cornmeal Waffles (page 107), with Totchos (page 108), in soup, or on sandwiches.

TARA'S TIP

Wash oranges and limes before juicing them to remove the wax, then add the juiced rinds to the marinade. You'll strain them out of the cooking juices later.

8 medium cloves garlic, minced

2 teaspoons ground cumin

1½ teaspoons ground black pepper

1½ teaspoons dried oregano

¾ cup low-sodium chicken broth

½ cup fresh orange juice

¼ cup fresh lime juice

2 tablespoons extra-virgin olive oil

1 teaspoon kosher salt

1 (6- to 8-pound) boneless pork shoulder roast, fat rind removed, tied with kitchen twine

2 cups water

1. In a large bowl or extra-large zip-top bag, combine the garlic, cumin, pepper, oregano, chicken broth, orange and lime juices, olive oil, and salt. Add pork roast. Cover bowl or seal bag and refrigerate at least 2 hours or overnight.
2. Transfer pork and marinade to a slow cooker. Add water and cook on high until pork is tender and shreds easily, 5½ to 6 hours.
3. Heat broiler to high and line a rimmed baking sheet with foil. Using a meat fork or tongs, transfer pork from slow cooker to the prepared baking sheet, reserving juices that are left behind. Broil roast, rotating as needed, until it is caramelized on all sides, 5 to 8 minutes. Let pork cool slightly.
4. Remove kitchen twine from pork and shred on baking sheet with 2 forks.
5. Strain reserved cooking juices into a bowl through a fine-mesh sieve and discard solids. Pour over shredded pork. Store leftover pork in mojo liquid, if desired.

the new york focaccia sandwich

ON MAGAZINE PHOTO SHOOTS in New York City, the crew would often order lunch at a place called Wichcraft. I was always happy when I could get this sandwich with the soup-of-the-day. The focaccia at Wichcraft was thinner—I like mine with a bit more loft to it (The Ultimate Focaccia)—but the layers are the same: a flavorful white bean spread, sundried tomatoes (I use my juicy Oven-Roasted Plum Tomatoes), peppery greens, nutty cheese, and very, very thinly sliced red onion.

These vegetarian-friendly sandwiches are perfect for a pool party, picnic, or beach day because there's no mayo or meat. Pack them individually or serve on a party platter.

2 cups Parmesan and Herb White Bean Dip (page 21)

1 recipe The Ultimate Focaccia (page 31)

1 recipe Oven-Roasted Plum Tomatoes (page 157)

5 cups (5 ounces) baby arugula

2 ounces Pecorino Romano or Parmesan, shaved

1 cup thinly sliced red onion

1. Cut focaccia into 18 2-by-3-inch squares. Slice horizontally to create tops and bottoms for each sandwich.

2. Spread 1 to 2 tablespoons Parmesan and Herb White Bean Dip on each slice of focaccia.

3. Layer bread with roasted tomato slices, arugula, shaved Pecorino, and sliced red onions. Top with remaining slices of focaccia.

MAKES

18 SANDWICHES

HANDS-ON TIME

20 MINUTES

TOTAL TIME

20 MINUTES NOT INCLUDING OTHER RECIPE PREPARATION

TARA'S TIP

Streamline these sandwiches by making the focaccia the day before. The bean dip and roasted tomatoes can also be made several days in advance and kept in the fridge until needed.

swedish meatballs with noodles and chutney

A FEW THINGS elevate this recipe above all other Swedish meatballs. The first is adding sour cream to the meat mixture, which makes the meatballs extra tender and adds that signature flavor to the dish without it going in the sauce. The second is the beautiful translucent gravy that gets its rich flavor from browning one helpful meatball in the pan, creating fond, or browned, bits. Deglaze the pan with a bit of piquant vinegar, and you have the base of a really delicious sauce. Caraway seeds, egg noodles, and loads of bright parsley lend authentic flavor to this take on a traditional dish.

MAKES

6 SERVINGS
(22 MEATBALLS)

HANDS-ON TIME

50 MINUTES

TOTAL TIME

1 HOUR 50 MINUTES

8 ounces ground pork

8 ounces ground sirloin

1 cup finely chopped yellow onion

¼ cup sour cream

1 large egg, lightly beaten

3 tablespoons fine dry breadcrumbs

1½ teaspoons kosher salt

⅛ teaspoon ground black pepper

½ teaspoon ground allspice

¼ teaspoon ground nutmeg

1 (16-ounce) package egg noodles

2 cups beef broth

2 tablespoons cornstarch

1 tablespoon olive oil

1 tablespoon red wine vinegar

3 tablespoons unsalted butter, melted

2 teaspoons caraway seeds

¼ cup coarsely chopped flat-leaf parsley

1 recipe Sweet and Savory Cranberry Chutney (page 160), prepared

> **TARA'S TIP**
>
> Instead of cooking all the meatballs in a skillet just to create flavor for the sauce, I add the step of browning one meatball in the pan, then baking the rest. It's my flavorful-sauce gift to you.
>
> Make a double batch and freeze meatballs for up to a month. Just add an extra 15 minutes onto the baking time.

1. In a large bowl, use clean or gloved hands to mix together pork, beef, onion, sour cream, egg, breadcrumbs, salt, pepper, allspice, and nutmeg until well combined. Shape into 23 1¼-inch balls. Reserve one meatball to use in sauce. Place remaining meatballs on a foil-lined, rimmed baking sheet and freeze 20 to 30 minutes. Remove from freezer and reroll each meatball in hands to make round again, if needed.

2. Heat oven to 350°F. Bake meatballs until browned and cooked through, about 30 minutes.

3. While meatballs are cooking, prepare noodles according to package directions. When meatballs are almost finished cooking, whisk together the broth and cornstarch in a medium bowl and set aside.

4. Heat oil in a medium saucepan over medium heat. Add reserved meatball and break up into small pieces. Let cook, stirring occasionally, until pieces are deep brown. Add the vinegar and deglaze the pan by scraping up browned bits. Cook until vinegar is almost evaporated. Whisk in reserved broth and cornstarch mixture. Bring to a simmer and stir until thickened, 3 to 4 minutes. Season with salt and pepper, to taste.

5. In a large bowl, toss cooked noodles with melted butter and caraway seeds. Serve noodles topped with meatballs, sauce, and plenty of chopped parsley. Serve with cranberry chutney.

MAKES

6 TO 8 SERVINGS

HANDS-ON TIME

15 MINUTES

TOTAL TIME

1 HOUR 45 MINUTES

herb-glazed fall-off-the-bone BBQ ribs

IF I WERE RUNNING in the BBQ circles of famous pit masters of the American South, they might notice I'm cheating. True pit masters tend their smoker starting in the wee hours of the morning and go all day long. While I have taken classes to be a certified barbecue judge (that's a thing, and it's a delicious task), I'm not the type of cook who wants to tend the grill, or smoker, for hours. I like my tender, fall-off-the-bone ribs lickety-split.

I use my versatile spice rub to add depth of flavor, then steam the ribs in the oven to tenderize them quickly. Char them on a hot grill, slather them with sweet, orangey glaze and you'll feel like a real pit master, even if you just play one in the kitchen.

TARA'S TIP

I use orange marmalade in my apricot glaze when I make it for these ribs, but it's just as delicious with apricot jam.

2 recipes Savory-Sweet Apricot Glaze (below), prepared (use orange marmalade instead of apricot jam)

5 pounds baby back ribs (2 racks)

6 tablespoons Go-To Steak Rub (page 103)

Rosemary, for garnish

1. Heat oven to 400°F and move rack to lower third of oven.
2. Pat ribs dry and place each rack of ribs on a sheet of heavy-duty aluminum foil large enough to wrap around ribs. Rub ribs on both sides with steak rub. Wrap in foil, making an airtight seal. Transfer to a rimmed baking sheet and roast 1 hour 30 minutes.
3. Heat grill to medium-high. Remove ribs from oven and foil. Grill, turning once, until grill-marked, 8 to 10 minutes. Generously brush with glaze and slice into portions. Serve with rosemary, if desired.

SAVORY-SWEET APRICOT GLAZE

MAKES

¾ CUP

HANDS-ON TIME

10 MINUTES

TOTAL TIME

10 MINUTES

A TRULY VERSATILE condiment! You can create different flavors simply by using different jams—I recommend orange marmalade, peach, or pineapple. I use this glaze on my Sweet Glazed Sausage Tartine with Greens (page 137). Try it on ribs, roast pork or tenderloin, chicken, as a spread for sandwiches, or as a condiment on cheese boards.

½ cup apricot jam

2 tablespoons sliced or finely diced red onion

1 tablespoon balsamic vinegar

¼ teaspoon kosher salt

½ teaspoon chopped fresh rosemary or thyme

Heat apricot jam in a small saucepan over medium heat until just hot. Stir in remaining ingredients and let cool. Store in refrigerator up to 5 days.

MORNING GLORIES

spanish tortilla with mushrooms and bacon

TORTILLAS IN SPAIN are not thin corn or flour flatbreads, but rather silky, potato-filled egg dishes, somewhat like a frittata. They are eaten throughout the day, and often a slice is served as a snack in the afternoon.

I've added mushrooms and bacon to mine, making it both breakfast and brunch-worthy. And although these additions make for a few extra steps in an already long process, they are, oh, so worth it.

Read through the directions before starting so you don't miss a step. And yes, the recipe really does call for ½ cup olive oil! The amount is necessary to make sure the potatoes are authentically cooked. Much of the excess oil is strained off later, and you can use it for other things.

MAKES

6 TO 8 SERVINGS

HANDS-ON TIME

1 HOUR

TOTAL TIME

1 HOUR 10 MINUTES

½ pound (about 7 slices) bacon

4 ounces shiitake mushrooms, sliced

7 large eggs

1½ teaspoons kosher salt

¼ teaspoon ground black pepper

½ cup extra-virgin olive oil

1½ pounds waxy potatoes, such as Yukon Gold, peeled, cut into quarters, and thinly sliced

½ medium yellow onion, thinly sliced root to tip

Chives, for garnish

Sour cream, for serving

1. Heat oven to 400°F. Place bacon strips on a foil-lined, rimmed baking sheet in an even layer. Bake until just crisp, 13 to 15 minutes. Remove from oven and transfer bacon strips to a paper-towel lined plate, reserving bacon fat in pan.

2. Spoon 1 tablespoon bacon fat from the baking sheet into a 10-inch nonstick skillet. Heat fat over medium-high heat and add mushrooms. Sauté mushrooms until slightly browned, about 5 minutes. Remove from skillet. Wipe skillet clean to use again.

3. Set aside ¼ cup of mushrooms and 2 slices of bacon for garnishing. Chop remaining bacon into ½-inch pieces and combine with the remaining mushrooms.

4. In another large bowl, break egg yolks and whites with a spatula or spoon, but do not beat the eggs. Stir in the chopped bacon-and-mushroom mixture, as well as the salt and pepper; set aside.

5. Heat olive oil in the cleaned skillet over medium-high heat. Add potatoes and onion. Use a heatproof spatula to flip and coat potatoes with oil. When oil begins to bubble, reduce heat to medium-low and cook, stirring frequently and gently, until potatoes are tender but not browned, 12 to 18 minutes. If the potatoes begin to break, they are overdone; stop cooking.

6. Drain potatoes in a colander that is set over a large bowl to catch the oil. Save oil to use in step 7. Gently stir potatoes into the eggs. Wipe skillet clean to use again.

7. Heat 3 tablespoons drained oil in the skillet over medium-high heat. Stir egg-and-potato mixture again, being careful not to break up potatoes, then add to

skillet. Cook, stirring constantly, until eggs begin to set, 2 to 3 minutes. Spread mixture in an even layer and reduce heat to medium-low; cover pan with a lid or foil and cook 5 minutes.

8. Run a rubber spatula around the edges to make sure tortilla will release from the pan; the top will still be runny. Slide the pan onto a cutting board or plate, cover with another plate or small cutting board, and flip it, inverting everything.

9. Add another 2 tablespoons of the reserved oil to the skillet and gently slide the tortilla back into the pan to cook the other side.

10. Cover pan again and cook 3 to 5 minutes. Slide the tortilla from the skillet onto a serving board or platter. Let rest 10 to 15 minutes and then serve warm or at room temperature, garnished with the reserved bacon and mushrooms, as well as some chives and sour cream. The tortilla can be left at room temperature up to 2 hours. After that, refrigerate the leftovers.

whole wheat pancakes

FORGET THE whole wheat flour, these hearty pancakes are made in a blender with whole wheat berries, which creates a glorious, soft-but-crunchy texture in the pancakes. They are straight from my grandmother's repertoire, and oh, how they remind me of childhood. Mornings at grandma's meant waking up to the sound of the blender and the smell of bacon. These melt-in-your-mouth pancakes were always on the menu.

I like to serve them with my Vanilla Bean Buttermilk Syrup, which comes together quickly and can be made ahead of time and then reheated while your pancakes are on the griddle.

MAKES

10 (4-INCH) PANCAKES

HANDS-ON TIME

15 MINUTES

TOTAL TIME

15 MINUTES

1 cup whole wheat berries	1 teaspoon baking soda
1 cup whole milk	¼ teaspoon salt
1 large egg	2 tablespoons granulated sugar
⅓ cup canola or avocado oil	Vanilla Bean Buttermilk Syrup (page 182)
2 teaspoons baking powder	

1. Combine wheat berries and milk in a blender. Blend on medium-high for 4 minutes.
2. Add egg, oil, baking powder, baking soda, salt, and sugar to the blender and blend 2 more minutes.
3. Heat a griddle or nonstick skillet over medium heat. Scoop batter, in ⅓-cup portions, onto the hot pan. Cook 1 minute, until a few bubbles pop and stay open; flip and cook 30 to 60 seconds more.
4. Serve pancakes hot with butter and syrup.

TARA'S TIP

I prefer to use hard red wheat, though these pancakes work fine with softer, white wheat and even kamut, an ancient grain. Use what you can find at your market.

If using a powerful blender like a Vitamix, Blendtec, or Ninja, blend the wheat and milk on #4 or #5 speed (medium). Keep the power on the lower speed for the second blend as well.

MAKES

2 CUPS

HANDS-ON TIME

5 MINUTES

TOTAL TIME

10 MINUTES

vanilla bean buttermilk syrup

I TOOK MY childhood-favorite syrup up a notch by adding vanilla bean. Use half a vanilla bean and save the other half for your next batch. This sweet cream buttermilk syrup is amazing for pancakes, waffles, scones, cakes, and anything else you can think of to put it on. (I love it on an apple cake in the fall.)

1½ cups granulated sugar

½ teaspoon salt

¾ cup buttermilk

½ cup unsalted butter

1 tablespoon light corn syrup

1 teaspoon baking soda

½ vanilla bean

1. In a large saucepan over medium-high heat, add sugar, salt, buttermilk, butter, corn syrup, and baking soda.
2. Slice vanilla bean in half lengthwise and scrape seeds into pan. Add scraped pod to pan as well.
3. Bring mixture to a boil, stirring often. Let mixture boil 30 seconds, then remove from heat. Remove vanilla bean pod when ready to serve.
4. Serve warm or store in the fridge up to a week. Warm slightly to serve again.

TARA'S TIP

Vanilla beans make this syrup special, but you can swap the bean for ½ teaspoon vanilla bean paste or 1 teaspoon vanilla extract.

Use a large saucepan because the baking soda bubbles up in reaction to the buttermilk; if your pan is small, the mixture may overflow.

MAKES

6 TO 8 SERVINGS

HANDS-ON TIME

10 MINUTES

TOTAL TIME

5 HOURS

slow-cooker almond and whole grain cereal

THIS IS A GLORIOUS make-ahead hot cereal for those mornings you don't want to slow-cook hearty grains. I keep a batch of this in the fridge, and heat it for breakfast throughout the week. Top it with seasonal fruit and, if you're like me, an extra drizzle of honey.

Use different grains, including kamut, spelt, or short-grain brown rice, to make it your own. This is a nice change from oats, and the crunchy nuts will have you gesturing for joy with jazz hands.

TARA'S TIP

Most slow cookers have a "keep warm" function after the cooking time is over, but this cereal will be overcooked if left in the slow cooker longer than 6 hours. If you are an early riser, you could make this an overnight recipe, but I like my sleep, so I make it during the day and store it for the next day's breakfast.

½ cup chopped raw almonds

½ cup whole wheat berries

½ cup pearled barley

½ cup red quinoa

5½ cups water

¾ teaspoon kosher salt

3 tablespoons agave or honey

Toppings, such as citrus, bananas, strawberries, coconut flakes, raspberries, figs, grapes, blueberries, blackberries, golden berries, or pomegranate arils

1. In a 4- or 6-quart slow cooker, stir together all ingredients except the toppings. Cover and cook on low 5 hours.

2. Serve hot with yogurt or milk, topped with fruit and extra nuts. Keep leftovers refrigerated up to a week and reheat to eat each morning.

cornmeal waffles with cinnamon-pecan maple syrup

SPICED CANDIED NUTS are fantastic. Cornbread is the best. Together, they are perfect pals at breakfast. The browned butter syrup with pecans is like liquefied, spiced, candied nuts, and the fluffy cornbread waffles are all my Southern dreams come true. I strongly suggest the dollop of tangy vanilla yogurt to complete this all-around transcendent breakfast.

MAKES

8 SQUARE WAFFLES, DEPENDING ON THE SIZE OF YOUR WAFFLE IRON

HANDS-ON TIME

25 MINUTES

TOTAL TIME

40 MINUTES

SYRUP

½ cup (1 stick) unsalted butter

¼ teaspoon salt

1½ cups pure maple syrup

1 cup coarsely chopped, toasted pecans

¼ teaspoon cayenne

1 teaspoon ground cinnamon

WAFFLES

1¼ cups all-purpose flour

¾ cup yellow cornmeal

¼ cup packed light brown sugar

1 tablespoon baking powder

½ teaspoon baking soda

½ teaspoon salt

2 large eggs

1 cup buttermilk

½ teaspoon vanilla extract

¼ cup canola or avocado oil

4 tablespoons unsalted butter, melted

Vanilla yogurt, for serving

TARA'S TIP

I use a standard waffle iron, but if you are using a round or Belgian-style waffle maker, adjust the quantity of batter for each section accordingly.

1. Make syrup: In a medium saucepan over medium heat, melt butter and salt and cook until browned and nutty smelling, stirring often, 4 to 6 minutes. Stir in maple syrup, pecans, cayenne, and cinnamon. Bring to a simmer, and simmer for 2 minutes. Remove from heat.

2. Make waffles: In a large bowl, whisk together flour, cornmeal, sugar, baking powder, baking soda, and remaining salt. In a separate bowl, whisk together eggs, buttermilk, oil, butter, and vanilla. Add egg mixture to flour mixture and stir just to combine.

3. Heat waffle iron, and ladle 1 to 2 cups batter into iron, depending on the style waffle iron you have. Cook until baked through and just turning golden, about 4 to 5 minutes. Place waffles in a warm oven to keep warm while you make the rest.

4. Serve with syrup and a dollop of vanilla yogurt.

mexican-spiced black-bean hash browns and eggs

MY TAKE ON HUEVOS RANCHEROS involves crispy hash brown potatoes instead of tortillas and seasoned with all the spices that make Mexican food delicious. It's a one-skillet meal filled with crispy and soft potatoes, black beans, eggs, and tasty fixings. I'll spare implicating anyone by name, but this breakfast often gets eaten right out of my pan before it gets to the table! (It's me; I do this. But I promise to play fair and share, if you invite me over.)

MAKES

4 TO 6 SERVINGS

HANDS-ON TIME

15 MINUTES

TOTAL TIME

35 MINUTES

3 tablespoons olive oil

2 tablespoons unsalted butter

1 (30-ounce package) frozen hash browns, partially thawed (6 cups)

½ cup finely chopped yellow onion

1 cup canned black beans, drained

¾ teaspoon ground cumin

¾ teaspoon dried oregano

½ teaspoon chili powder

1 teaspoon kosher salt

½ small jalapeño, seeded and finely chopped

4 large eggs

Toppings, such as salsa, cherry tomatoes, cilantro, diced avocado, and cotija cheese

> **TARA'S TIP**
>
> The presentation of the eggs cooked in the hash browns is fun, but you can skip that step and serve the hash browns with fried or scrambled eggs on the side. It will serve up to 6 people as a side.

1. Heat oil and butter in a large 12- or 14-inch nonstick skillet over medium-high heat until butter melts. Add thawed hash browns and onion and stir to coat. Cook 5 to 7 minutes, until just starting to crisp. Stir in cumin, oregano, chili powder, salt, and jalapeño and cook 4 to 6 minutes, until potatoes start to brown and crisp.

2. Reduce heat to medium. Stir in black beans and then make 4 wells in the potato mixture. Crack 1 egg in each well, cover pan with lid, and cook eggs to desired doneness, about 10 minutes for soft eggs.

3. Divide hash browns and eggs between 4 plates and serve immediately with your favorite toppings.

MAKES

10 LARGE MUFFINS

HANDS-ON TIME

25 MINUTES

TOTAL TIME

1 HOUR 20 MINUTES

giant and glorious blueberry streusel muffins

A LARGER-THAN-LIFE breakfast muffin is a welcome morning treat, and these are as grand as you can get. They perfectly rise out of the tin and ascend to the highest of blueberry-streusel heights. A warm bite, slathered with generous amounts of butter, is one of the many rewards for making your own muffins at home.

I love baking a classic blueberry muffin in large tins so there is plenty of the tender, cakey muffin inside, speckled with juicy berries. The giant muffin top—the best part, of course—has more surface area for the sweet, buttery streusel topping. And here's a luscious little tip: swap chopped fresh peaches in for blueberries when they're in season.

TARA'S TIP

The muffins are at their best when freshly made, but they can be stored in an airtight container or zip-top bag for a day or two.

STREUSEL TOPPING

1 cup all-purpose flour

¼ cup light brown sugar

1 teaspoon ground cinnamon

¼ teaspoon salt

6 tablespoons unsalted butter, at room temperature

MUFFINS

3 cups, plus 2 tablespoons all-purpose flour

1 tablespoon baking powder

1½ teaspoons salt

6 tablespoons unsalted butter, softened

1¾ cups granulated sugar

1 large egg

2 large egg yolks

1 teaspoon vanilla extract

1 cup whole milk

2 cups (10 ounces) fresh or frozen blueberries

1. Make streusel topping: In a medium bowl, whisk together flour, sugar, cinnamon, and salt. Cut in the butter using a pastry blender or fork until fine crumbs form. Using your hands, squeeze together the mixture to form large clumps. Store, refrigerated, until ready to use.

2. Make muffins: Heat oven to 375°F. Line 2 large muffin tins (3½-inch cups) with 10 large muffin papers.

3. In a large bowl, whisk together flour, baking powder, and salt; set aside. In the bowl of an electric mixer fitted with the paddle attachment, cream butter and sugar on medium speed until smooth and light, about 3 minutes.

4. Add egg, egg yolks, and vanilla, and mix until well combined. Gradually mix in flour mixture, alternating with the milk, and mixing between each addition, beginning and ending with flour.

5. Remove bowl from mixer and gently fold in blueberries. Divide batter between muffin cups. Each cup should have about ½ cup batter. Distribute streusel topping among muffins, gently pressing onto batter.

6. Bake until light golden and cooked through, 38 to 45 minutes. Cool in pan 15 minutes and then remove to a cooling rack.

the perfect cluster granola

GRANOLA TYPICALLY INVOLVES a tasty base of oats, nuts, coconut, seeds, and crunchies, bound together with sweetness and spice. With this recipe, once you have the foundation, it's easy to switch up the flavors, depending on what you love. Replace coconut sugar for the brown sugar, add more spices, such as nutmeg or ginger, or swap in different nuts, like pepitas or hazelnuts. Breakfast is too serious a matter to settle for anything but the best version!

I blend a bit of my oats into flour to create structure, then add a touch of leavening and my secret sauce: brown rice syrup. These tricks make the granola cookie-like, but without the eggs and all-purpose flour. You get large pieces so it's also great for a handy snack.

I don't include dried fruit in my granola because I find it gets too chewy. But I love adding fresh fruit on top, and I'll use whatever is in season.

MAKES

6 TO 8 (½-CUP) SERVINGS

HANDS-ON TIME

40 MINUTES

TOTAL TIME

1 HOUR 30 MINUTES

4 cups rolled oats, divided	1 cup Rice Krispies cereal
¼ cup roughly chopped almonds	2 tablespoons flaxseeds
½ cup roughly chopped pecans	1¼ teaspoons ground cinnamon
½ cup roughly chopped walnuts	½ cup coconut oil
½ cup unsweetened large-flaked coconut	½ cup light brown sugar
1 teaspoon baking soda	2 tablespoons plus 1 teaspoon brown rice syrup
¾ teaspoon kosher salt	½ cup unsweetened applesauce
½ cup wheat germ	

1. Heat oven to 325°F. Process 1 cup of the oats in a small food processor or blender until it turns into a fine powder. In a large bowl, combine powdered oats with the remaining oats, nuts, and coconut. Stir in baking soda, salt, wheat germ, Rice Krispies cereal, flaxseeds, and cinnamon; set aside.

2. In a medium, microwave-safe bowl combine the coconut oil, brown sugar, brown rice syrup, and applesauce. Heat on high until coconut oil is melted and mixture is hot, about 1 minute. Stir well, then pour over oat mixture. Stir 2 minutes to coat everything.

3. On a parchment-lined baking sheet, gently press granola to flatten and evenly distribute it. Use another piece of parchment between the granola and your hand to press it down.

4. Bake 15 minutes then reduce oven temperature to 250°F, rotate pan, and bake until granola is deep golden and almost dry, another 30 to 35 minutes. Cool completely on pan and then break up into pieces and store in an airtight container. Granola can be stored up to a month.

TARA'S TIP

You can find brown rice syrup in your health food store or online. It acts as a subtle sweetener, but because it's a liquid form of sugar that's not overly processed, it gives the granola a light and crisp texture.

My trick: oil your measuring spoons before using them for the syrup to avoid a sticky mess.

SWEETS TO SHARE

my favorite coconut cream pie

THERE'S A REASON a food holiday exists that features pie as the main dessert. Pie is everything! You won't see me waiting for Thanksgiving to make custard-filled, buttery-crust comfort though. This nostalgic dessert is a take on my mom's beloved coconut pie, and one of my childhood favorites. I've added coconut milk to the easy-to-make custard for an intense flavor. Use my All-Butter Double-Crust Pastry, add some lofty whipped cream on top, and you'll have a cream pie dessert that just might become your favorite too.

MAKES

8 SERVINGS

HANDS-ON TIME

15 MINUTES

TOTAL TIME

5 HOURS,
15 MINUTES

½ recipe All-Butter Double-Crust Pastry (page 198)

⅔ cup granulated sugar

¼ teaspoon salt

5 tablespoons cornstarch

1 cup full-fat unsweetened coconut milk

1 cup half-and-half

4 large egg yolks

½ cup boiling water

1 tablespoon unsalted butter

1½ teaspoons coconut extract

1½ cups heavy cream

¾ cup confectioners' sugar

1 teaspoon vanilla extract

⅓ cup large-flake coconut, toasted

> **TARA'S TIP**
> To toast coconut, bake it on a baking sheet in a 350°F oven for 5 to 7 minutes, until light brown in parts. Let cool.

1. Use the blind bake instructions for the All-Butter Double-Crust Pastry, baking crust in a 9-inch pie pan. Set aside.

2. In a heavy saucepan, whisk together sugar, salt, and cornstarch. Stir in coconut milk and half-and-half and whisk to combine. Whisk in the egg yolks until mixture is thoroughly combined.

3. Place the pan over medium-high heat. Whisk constantly as mixture cooks. When warm, reduce heat to medium and stir in boiling water. Continue stirring until mixture bubbles; this will take 5 to 7 minutes. Let bubble 1 minute and then remove from heat and add butter and coconut extract. Whisk until butter is melted.

4. Cover the surface of custard with plastic wrap and allow to cool almost to room temperature, about 1 hour. Pour into baked pastry shell. Recover pie with plastic wrap and chill until set, 4 hours.

5. In a large bowl, whip together cream, vanilla extract, and confectioners' sugar with an electric mixer on high speed until firm peaks form. Top pie with whipped cream and garnish with toasted coconut flakes.

LOOKS DELICIOUS I used a 9-inch pastry ring for this pie. It is a stainless steel, open ring for baking or frozen desserts, and you can find them at baking supply stores. However, a standard 9-inch pie pan will do as well; you'll just want to crimp the edges of the crust to look pretty.

I pipe my whipped cream on top using an Ateco #867 open star tip.

MAKES

2 SINGLE CRUSTS

HANDS-ON TIME

20 MINUTES

TOTAL TIME

45 MINUTES

ALL-BUTTER DOUBLE-CRUST PASTRY

THIS BASIC PÂTE BRISÉE recipe turns out flaky and flavorful crusts. I add vinegar to this classic French pastry dough to help tenderize the buttery crumb. It's a great recipe that complements all sorts of fillings for pies and tarts, both savory and sweet. This recipe makes two single crusts; if you are using only one, the other can be chilled up to a week or frozen up to a month.

½ cup ice water

1 tablespoon white vinegar

2½ cups all-purpose flour

1 cup cold unsalted butter, cut into ½-inch cubes

1 teaspoon salt

1 teaspoon granulated sugar

1. Mix together the ice water and vinegar; set aside.
2. Mix flour, sugar, and salt in a food processor. Add butter and pulse until butter is the size of peas. Add ⅓ cup water-vinegar mixture in a slow stream and pulse several times. Pinch dough to see if it is holding together. If it's not, add more water, 1 tablespoon at a time, pulsing once or twice after each addition, until the dough just holds together.
3. Working quickly so the butter doesn't soften, gather dough together and divide in half. Form dough into two disks, wrap each disk in plastic wrap, and chill 30 minutes or overnight.

BLIND-BAKED SINGLE-CRUST

1. Heat oven to 375°F. On a floured work surface, roll one single crust to about 12-inches diameter. Transfer dough to a 9-inch pie plate or tart pan with removable bottom. Trim edges so they hang ½-inch over the lip of the pie plate. Tuck overhang under itself and crimp edges as desired.
2. Freeze crust for 20 minutes. Line frozen crust with a circle of parchment larger than pie pan, and fill with baking beans or baking weights. Bake 20 to 30 minutes, until edges begin to brown.
3. Carefully remove parchment with beans and bake an additional 10 to 15 minutes, until the center of the crust turns light golden brown.
4. Let cool before filling.

RICH CREAM CHEESE FROSTING

THIS FROSTING is a classic, so why change perfection? I use this on a variety of cookies and cakes, and it is always delicious. This recipe makes enough to frost a 9-by-13-inch sheet cake or 24 cupcakes.

1 (8-ounce) package cream cheese, softened

½ cup unsalted butter, softened

1 teaspoon vanilla extract

Pinch salt

4 cups confectioners' sugar, sifted

1. In the bowl of an electric mixer fitted with the paddle attachment, beat cream cheese until smooth. Add the butter and beat until smooth and incorporated, about 1 minute. Add the vanilla and salt and mix briefly.

2. With the mixer running on low speed, add the confectioners' sugar ½ cup at a time. After each cup or cup and a half, turn off mixer, scrape down the inside of the bowl with a rubber spatula, and then turn mixer to medium-high speed for 10 to 15 seconds. Reduce speed to low and add more sugar. Repeat until all sugar has been added. This will ensure a smooth frosting.

3. Use frosting immediately or keep refrigerated in an airtight container up to a week. To use again, bring almost to room temperature and beat until smooth.

LOOKS DELICIOUS If you want to pipe a design on your frosted cupcakes or frost a round layer cake cake (like the Mulling-Spice Christmas Tree Cake on page 228), increase the amounts by 1½, to 12 ounces cream cheese, ¾ cup unsalted butter, 6 cups confectioners' sugar, and 1½ teaspoons vanilla.

MAKES

2½ CUPS FROSTING

HANDS-ON TIME

10 MINUTES

TOTAL TIME

10 MINUTES

SWEETS TO SHARE

vanilla sour cream pound cake

MAKES

12 TO 15 SERVINGS

HANDS-ON TIME

15 MINUTES

TOTAL TIME

1 HOUR 45 MINUTES

THIS GLORIOUS butter and sour cream cake has an ultra-fine and tender crumb and is lovely baked in a Bundt pan or a decorative tube pan. I've added generous amounts of vanilla to make it perfect for eating on its own, topped with sliced strawberries or peaches to make a shortcake, or served with warm vanilla pudding and cold whipped cream—an updated version of one of my favorite childhood desserts.

1 cup unsalted butter, at room temperature, plus more for pan

2¾ cups granulated sugar, plus more for pan

3 cups all-purpose flour

1 teaspoon salt

¼ teaspoon baking soda

1 tablespoon vanilla extract

6 large eggs

1 cup sour cream

1. Heat oven to 325°F. and adjust rack to middle position. Generously butter a 10-cup Bundt or tube pan, using a pastry brush to spread butter to all the nooks and crevices of the pan. Sprinkle the inside with extra sugar, tapping out excess; set aside.

2. In a large bowl, whisk together flour, salt, and baking soda; set aside. In the bowl of an electric mixer fitted with the paddle attachment, cream butter and sugar until light and fluffy, about 2 minutes. Mix in vanilla. Add eggs, one at a time, mixing between each addition. Scrape down the inside of the bowl as needed to keep everything mixed evenly.

3. Add flour mixture alternately with the sour cream in three batches, starting and ending with flour. After the last addition, beat on high speed 10 seconds.

4. Transfer batter to prepared pan and bake until a toothpick inserted into the center comes out clean, about 1 hour.

5. Let cake cool in pan ten minutes, then turn out onto a wire rack to cool completely. Cake can be stored, covered, up to 3 days.

TARA'S TIP

A classic Bundt recipe is typically baked in a 10-cup capacity pan, but Bundt pans come in an array of sizes, so if you are unsure of the size of your pan, use water to measure the cup capacity.

For a fun variation, replace the vanilla with 1 teaspoon each orange and lemon extracts.

LOOKS DELICIOUS Brushing the inside of the pan with soft butter and coating it with sugar creates a nonstick surface for the cake as well as resulting in a subtle and gratifying sugary crust. Make sure to get the butter in every crevice of the pan with your pastry brush to create the air pockets needed to release the cake beautifully.

MAKES

4 TO 6 SERVINGS

HANDS-ON TIME

15 MINUTES

TOTAL TIME

15 MINUTES

classic vanilla pudding

WHETHER YOU'RE EATING it straight out of a little dish with a spoon or dolloping it over pound cake, vanilla pudding is simply divine. It's the start of all goodness, the base of all things custardy and delicious, and can transport you to the best times of childhood. If you have a vanilla bean on hand, scrape the inside of it into the pudding when adding the half-and-half. Add the pod as well, and remove it when finished. It's a decadent treat in place of the vanilla extract.

⅔ cup granulated sugar	3 large egg yolks
¼ teaspoon salt	¾ cup boiling water
3 tablespoons cornstarch	1 tablespoon unsalted butter
1¾ cup half-and-half	1½ teaspoons vanilla extract

1. In a heavy saucepan, whisk together sugar, salt, and cornstarch. Stir in half-and-half and whisk well to combine. Whisk in the egg yolks until mixture is thoroughly combined.
2. Place the pan over medium-high heat. Whisk constantly as mixture cooks. When warm, reduce heat to medium and stir in boiling water. Continue stirring until mixture bubbles. Let bubble 1 minute, while stirring, and then remove from heat and add butter and vanilla extract. Whisk until butter is melted.
3. Serve or portion into small dishes. Cover top with plastic wrap to chill.

TARA'S TIP

If you are making this to serve with my rich Vanilla Sour Cream Pound Cake (page 201), you may want to double the recipe.

i promise you like blueberry pie

THIS PIE HAS CREATED more converts to blueberry pies than I can count. After just one bite, you'll have a table full of blueberry pie devotees. Make this with fresh or frozen blueberries, fresh lemon zest and juice, and a homemade pie crust. The simple flavors combine to make a truly spectacular dessert. I insist you have a scoop of vanilla ice cream with it. You decide if it goes on top or on the side!

MAKES

8 TO 10 SERVINGS

HANDS-ON TIME

30 MINUTES

TOTAL TIME

5 HOURS
30 MINUTES

1 recipe All-Butter Double-Crust Pastry (page 198)

6 cups (3 pints) fresh or frozen blueberries

¾ cup granulated sugar, plus more for top

1 teaspoon lemon zest

¼ cup fresh lemon juice

¼ teaspoon salt

⅓ cup cornstarch

2 tablespoons unsalted butter, melted

1 large egg

1 tablespoon water

TARA'S TIP

If you're using frozen blueberries, add an extra tablespoon cornstarch, and bake for an additional 10 to 15 minutes.

1. On a lightly floured surface, roll one chilled disk of All-Butter Double-Crust Pastry into a 13-inch circle. Gently fit into a deep (at least 1¾ inches tall) 9-inch pie dish. Trim overhang so there is at least a half inch hanging over the outside edge of the dish. Place in freezer while preparing filling. Keep second disk in refrigerator until you are ready to roll out the top crust.

2. Heat oven to 425°F and adjust rack to the lower third of the oven.

3. In a large bowl, toss blueberries with sugar, lemon zest, lemon juice, salt, cornstarch, and melted butter; set aside. Make an egg wash by beating the egg with 1 tablespoon of water in a small bowl; set aside.

4. On a lightly floured surface roll second piece of dough into an 11-by-15-inch rectangle. Cut into about 14 strips. Remove pie dish from freezer and fill with blueberry filling. Brush crust's edge with egg wash to act like glue.

5. Make a lattice top: Lay half of the strips of dough across the top of the pie, leaving about 1 inch between each strip. Fold back every other strip and lay down a strip across them. Unfold the strips that were folded over and fold back the other strips. Lay another strip across. Continue this process across the pie.

6. Using kitchen shears, trim excess crust from edges. Fold rough dough edges under to form a rim and pinch to form a ruffled crust edge. Brush pie with egg wash and sprinkle generously with extra sugar.

7. Place pie on a parchment-lined baking sheet and bake 15 minutes. Reduce oven temperature to 375°F and bake until juices are bubbling and crust is golden brown, 45 to 55 minutes more. If needed, cover crust edges and spots with foil to prevent overbrowning.

8. Let pie cool on a wire rack at least 4 hours or up to 6 before serving to let filling set. If you like warm pie, you can reheat cooled pie in a 350°F oven for 15 minutes before serving.

LOOKS DELICIOUS Experiment with your top crust. This pie is perfect for a lattice top, but you can also cover it with a full top crust and cut a few vent holes. Blueberries like to let off a lot of steam as they cook down.

MAKES

2 DOZEN
COOKIE BARS

HANDS-ON TIME

25 MINUTES

TOTAL TIME

1 HOUR

TARA'S TIP

To get the ½ cup ground almonds called for in the recipe, blend about ¾ cup sliced almonds in the food processor.

almond flower sugar cookie bars

THIS RECIPE takes a soft, buttery sugar cookie dough and transforms it into a fabulous bar with sweet ground almonds and almond extract. I like to blend my own almonds instead of using store-bought almond flour because it adds more almond flavor and gives the bars a nice, soft texture. Baking sugar cookies in bar form is one of my greatest joys. No rolling and cutting with shapes, and you get the same soft, sugar-cookie-eating-pleasure from a soft, cakey square with buttery frosting! The darling flowers on top are just to show off to your friends.

2¼ cups all-purpose flour

½ cup sliced almonds, finely ground, plus more almonds for flowers

½ teaspoon baking powder

½ teaspoon salt

½ cup (1 stick) unsalted butter, softened

1 cup granulated sugar

1 large egg

1 large egg white

2 tablespoons sour cream

2 teaspoons almond extract, divided

1 recipe Rich Cream Cheese Frosting (page 199)

24 colored candies, such as Sixlets or M&M's

1. Heat oven to 350°F. Line a 9-by-13-inch pan, or quarter-sheet pan, with parchment, allowing edges to hang over opposite sides.

2. In a large bowl, whisk together flour, ground almonds, baking powder, and salt; set aside. In the bowl of an electric mixer fitted with the paddle attachment, beat together butter and sugar until light and fluffy. Add egg, egg white, sour cream, and 1 teaspoon almond extract and mix until blended. Add flour mixture and mix on low speed until just combined and dough forms.

3. With greased hands, gently press dough into prepared pan. Bake until the edges are lightly golden, 17 to 19 minutes. Cool completely.

4. Stir 1 teaspoon almond extract into Cream Cheese Frosting. Frost cookie bars. With a knife, gently score the frosting to make 24 squares. While frosting is still soft, make flowers on each square using 5 or 6 sliced almonds. (I like to put the pointed, or tapered, end of the almond in the frosting so the fatter end becomes the flower petal). Add a colored candy to the center of each almond flower. Use the parchment overhang to lift from pan, slice, and serve.

bakery-style chocolate chunk cookies

MAKES

15 COOKIES

HANDS-ON TIME

15 MINUTES

TOTAL TIME

24 HOURS

SOMETIMES I JUST want a chocolate chip cookie the size of my face! And these cookies fit the bill! The secret-ingredient addition of cream cheese makes the cookies extra soft and rich. Plus, chilling the dough for twenty-four hours in the refrigerator allows the flour to absorb all the moisture, which creates a deliciously chewy cookie.

You can use chocolate chips, but I prefer to chop chocolate bars (both milk and semi-sweet) into big ½-inch chunks for these larger-than-life cookies. And I make them the way I love a chocolate chip cookie: with just enough cookie dough to hold the chocolate together!

1 cup, plus 5 tablespoons unsalted butter, softened

3 tablespoons cream cheese, softened

1 tablespoon molasses (not blackstrap)

1½ cups packed dark brown sugar

1 cup granulated sugar

2 large eggs

1 tablespoon vanilla extract

1½ teaspoons salt

1 teaspoon baking soda

4 cups all-purpose flour

2 cups (10 ounces) large milk chocolate chunks

2 cups (10 ounces) large semi-sweet chocolate chunks

Sea salt flakes (optional)

1. In a large bowl, cream together butter, cream cheese, molasses, and sugars with an electric mixer with a paddle attachment until softened and smooth, about 1 minute. Add eggs and vanilla and mix. Add the salt, baking soda, and flour and mix on low speed until all are incorporated. Scrape the sides and bottom of the bowl with a rubber spatula so that the dough is mixed evenly.

2. Stir in the chocolate chunks. Portion dough into 15 (5-ounce) balls—½- to ¾-cup size. Flatten just slightly. Place on a baking sheet and wrap with plastic wrap or place dough balls in a resealable gallon-size plastic bag. Chill at least 24 hours or up to 3 days.

3. When ready to bake, heat oven to 350°F. Place chilled dough balls on a parchment-lined baking sheet, at least 2 inches apart. Sprinkle with sea salt flakes, if desired. Bake until cookies are just setting and turning golden around the edges, 12 to 15 minutes. Don't overcook! Cookies will continue baking on the pan out of the oven. Let cookies cool completely (if you can wait) on the pan before removing.

MAKES

32 WHOOPIE PIES

HANDS-ON TIME

45 MINUTES

TOTAL TIME

1 HOUR
30 MINUTES

decadent chocolate-peanut butter whoopie pies

I'VE BEEN MAKING whoopie pies forever it seems. I know these treats are traditionally quite large, and I mean no offense to the Pennsylvania Amish and the state of Maine (both lay claim to the cookie's origin), but a mini-size just seems right to me. There's a fantastic balance between filling and cakey cookie when they're small.

I prefer my silky, rich, not-too-sweet Vanilla Swiss Meringue Buttercream instead of marshmallow crème or a confectioners' sugar fluff as the filling, but here I went totally off the rails with a peanut butter and chocolate combo, adding melty ganache and some disco lights in the form of gold sprinkles.

4 ounces semisweet chocolate,
  chopped (I use 60% cacao)

⅓ cup heavy cream

¾ cup unsweetened cocoa powder

1⅔ cups all-purpose flour

1 teaspoon baking soda

½ teaspoon salt

¼ cup unsalted butter, softened

¼ cup vegetable shortening

½ cup granulated sugar

½ cup packed light brown sugar

1 large egg

1 teaspoon vanilla extract

1 cup whole milk

1 recipe Swiss Meringue Buttercream, Peanut Butter Variation (page 235), prepared

Peanuts, crushed

Gold sprinkles

TARA'S TIP

If your ganache sets too firm before you use it, heat it slowly in the microwave or in a double boiler until soft and spreadable. Don't overheat or it will melt the buttercream.

1. Place chopped chocolate in a medium bowl and set aside. In a small saucepan or the microwave, heat cream until just simmering. Pour hot cream over chocolate in the bowl. Do not stir. Let sit 5 minutes and then stir until the chocolate is melted and mixture is smooth. Cover and set aside.

2. Heat oven to 375°F. Line three cookie sheets with parchment. Dip a 1½-inch round cookie cutter in extra cocoa powder and tap onto parchment to create a cookie outline; repeat to make a total of 32 outlines, 1-inch apart, on the baking sheets; set aside.

3. In a large bowl, whisk together cocoa powder, flour, baking soda, and salt; set aside. In the bowl of an electric mixer fitted with the paddle attachment, beat together the butter, shortening, and sugars on medium speed until smooth, about 2 minutes. Add egg and vanilla and beat until fluffy, about 2 more minutes. Stir in half of the flour mixture, then the milk, and beat to combine. Add remaining flour mixture and beat together, scraping down sides of bowl so everything is mixed evenly.

4. Transfer batter to a large piping bag fitted with a coupler or a ½-inch plain tip. Pipe onto parchment, filling the outlines with mounds about ½-inch high. Bake, one sheet at a time, until cookies spring back to the touch, 10 to 12 minutes. Cool on baking sheets 10 minutes, then transfer cookies to a wire rack to cool completely.

5. When cookies have cooled completely, spread or pipe about 1 tablespoon peanut butter buttercream on the flat side of half of the cookies. Spoon 1 to 2 teaspoons ganache on the flat side of the other half of the cookies and sandwich the cookies together. Repeat until all cookies have been used.

6. Spread a dab of ganache on the top of each cookie and top with sprinkles and peanuts.

MAKES

ABOUT 1½ PINTS

HANDS-ON TIME

45 MINUTES

TOTAL TIME

24 HOURS

SWEETS TO SHARE

212

strawberry cheesecake ice cream with gingersnaps

THERE ISN'T A homemade ice cream flavor I don't like, but cheesecake is one of my favorites. It's more fun than plain vanilla, and the addition of cookies and strawberry is pretty dreamy. The cookies get soft and cakey after freezing with the cream for a few hours, which is perfect bliss. You'll need an ice cream maker for this recipe, but if you don't have a fancy electric one, the kind where you freeze the bowl and then let the ice cream churn is great.

TARA'S TIP

Homemade ice cream base needs to chill and mellow for proper consistency, so make sure to chill it overnight in the refrigerator before churning. If ice cream is churned before it is cold, the formed ice crystals will be large and create a rougher texture. You can speed up this process by stirring the base over an ice bath until cold, but letting it chill overnight in the fridge is well worth the hands-off time.

1 cup granulated sugar, divided

4 ounces cream cheese, room temperature

½ cup crème fraîche

1 large egg

½ teaspoon vanilla extract

¾ cup whole milk

1 cup heavy cream

1¾ cups frozen strawberries, partially thawed and chopped

1 tablespoon fresh lemon juice

2 teaspoons cornstarch

1½ cups gingersnap cookie bits

1. In the bowl of an electric mixer fitted with the paddle attachment, beat together ¾ cup of sugar, cream cheese, and crème fraîche until smooth. Add the egg and vanilla and mix to combine. Set aside.

2. In a medium saucepan over medium heat, bring milk and cream to a low simmer. With the mixer on low, add half the warm milk to the cream cheese mixture and blend; then add this mixture back to the remaining milk in the saucepan. Whisk constantly over medium heat until mixture is thick, 4 to 5 minutes. Do not boil.

3. Strain mixture through sieve into a medium bowl and then set mixture over an ice bath until cool, 15 minutes. Once cool, transfer to an airtight container and refrigerate at least 5 hours or overnight.

4. In a small saucepan, combine cornstarch and remaining sugar. Add lemon juice and berries; lightly mash. Cook over medium heat, stirring frequently, until just bubbling, then reduce heat and simmer 2 minutes until mixture is thick and translucent. Remove from heat and cool completely. Store in the fridge until ready to use in ice cream.

5. Churn ice cream according to your machine's instructions, adding the cookie bits during the last few churns. Spread about ⅓ of the ice cream in a freezer container and top with strawberry sauce. Add another layer of ice cream and top with remaining sauce. Layer any remaining ice cream and freeze 4 hours or overnight before serving.

LOOKS DELICIOUS This treat is still glorious even if you don't make homemade ice cream! Start with 2 cups high-quality vanilla ice cream—I like Tillamook because it's made with extra cream so it's the texture of homemade—and scoop it into a stand mixer. Blend quickly with the paddle attachment to soften. Stir in prepared strawberry mixture and gingersnaps. Transfer to a container and freeze until solid..

coconut crunch flowers
ice cream sundaes

MY TAKE ON fried ice cream involves rolling the vanilla ice cream in a toasted coconut, crunchy coating. The honey and corn flakes make it delicious, and you could stop there, but adding fruit flower petals makes this fun ice cream sundae extra sweet.

MAKES

4 SUNDAES

HANDS-ON TIME

20 MINUTES

TOTAL TIME

40 MINUTES

3 tablespoons honey

2 tablespoons water

1 teaspoon vanilla extract

¾ cup shredded sweetened coconut flakes, lightly toasted

¾ cup corn flakes cereal

2 pints vanilla ice cream

Bananas, sliced on bias

Sliced strawberries

Maraschino cherries, drained

Sweetened whipped cream

Sprinkles

1. In a small saucepan over medium-high heat, bring honey and 2 tablespoons water to a boil. Boil for 2 minutes, then remove from heat and stir in vanilla. Mix in coconut and corn flakes until well coated. Pour mixture onto a sheet of parchment and let it cool completely, 20 minutes. Once cool, transfer to a gallon-sized, resealable bag. Seal bag and then use your hands or a rolling pin to crush the mixture to small crumbs.

2. Arrange fruit slices in 4 small bowls, lining them along the edge so they stand up like petals. Set aside.

3. With an ice cream scoop, form ¾-cup-sized balls of ice cream. Roll scoops of vanilla ice cream in coconut coating. Serve immediately or place on a parchment-lined baking sheet and freeze for up to 4 hours.

4. Add ice cream to bowls and top with whipped cream and sprinkles.

TARA'S TIP

Since ice cream can melt easily, I make sure to use a high-quality vanilla ice cream. Tillamook ice cream is made with extra cream so it's dense and luscious rather than overly-aerated like other brands. That consistency works perfectly for this sundae.

To toast coconut, bake it on a baking sheet in a 350°F oven for 5 to 7 minutes, until light brown in parts. Let cool.

LOOKS DELICIOUS Prepare your fruit bowls just prior to serving. You can also fill the bottom of the bowls with some crushed cookies, extra coconut, or even marshmallows to help hold the slices up along the sides.

MAKES

8 TO 10 SERVINGS

HANDS-ON TIME

25 MINUTES

TOTAL TIME

1 HOUR
45 MINUTES

pistachio cake with yogurt and citrus

THIS RECIPE WAS INSPIRED by a cake I found in an old cookbook by Maida Heatter, the queen of desserts! I made some tweaks and created two other variations using other nuts. This pistachio version is perfect as a special dessert, topped with vanilla yogurt and juicy orange segments, while still retaining a casual but refined presentation.

I omitted the salt in the recipe because the salted pistachios provide enough for the right flavor.

1¼ cups roasted and salted pistachios, shelled, plus more for garnish

1 cup plus 1 tablespoon granulated sugar, divided

1 cup sifted all-purpose flour

½ teaspoon baking powder

¼ teaspoon ground nutmeg

½ cup (1 stick) unsalted butter, softened

3 large eggs

1½ teaspoons vanilla extract

1 tablespoon honey

3 oranges, peeled and cut into segments, juice reserved (½ cup)

2 cups vanilla yogurt

1. Heat oven to 325°F. Butter an 8-inch round pan and line bottom with parchment. Grease bottom of parchment and sides of pan; set aside.
2. In a food processor, combine ¼ cup pistachios and 1 tablespoon sugar. Process until mixture resembles very fine crumbs; remove and set aside until just before baking cake. Pulse remaining 1 cup pistachios in food processor until finely chopped and some pea-sized pieces remain; set aside in a separate bowl.
3. In a large bowl, whisk together flour, baking powder, and nutmeg; set aside. In the bowl of an electric mixer fitted with the paddle attachment, beat together the butter and remaining 1 cup sugar until smooth. With the mixer on medium speed, add eggs, 1 at a time, beating to incorporate after each addition. Increase speed to medium-high and beat 1 minute more after adding the last egg so the mixture is light and fluffy. Stir in vanilla. Blend in the flour mixture just until incorporated. Add pulsed pistachios and stir them in.
4. Spread batter evenly into the prepared pan and sprinkle top with the reserved sugar and pistachio crumbs. Bake until a toothpick inserted in the center comes out clean, about 50 to 55 minutes. Let cool in pan, then gently remove.
5. For the glaze, combine reserved orange juice and honey in a small saucepan and bring to a simmer. Remove from heat and cool.
6. Top cake with dollops of yogurt, followed by orange segments. Garnish generously with extra chopped pistachios and drizzle glaze over all.

LOOKS DELICIOUS A rich Icelandic or Australian yogurt is my favorite with this cake, but even vanilla Greek yogurt is tasty. You can use any citrus on the cake, including blood oranges, caracara, or tangerines to change up the look and flavor of this dish.

walnut cake with maple cream cheese frosting

MAKES

8 TO 10 SERVINGS

HANDS-ON TIME

25 MINUTES

TOTAL TIME

1 HOUR
35 MINUTES

I LOVE SINGLE-LAYER CAKES because it makes me feel like I'm having a snack instead of a grand dessert. Plus, single-layer cakes have endless options for flavors. For this one, I used a maple frosting instead of a sugared top and it's divine.

CAKE

1 cup walnuts, plus more for garnish

1 cup sifted all-purpose flour

½ teaspoon baking powder

½ teaspoon salt

¼ teaspoon ground nutmeg

½ cup (1 stick) unsalted butter, softened

1 cup granulated sugar

3 large eggs

1½ teaspoons vanilla extract

FROSTING

4 ounces cream cheese, at room temperature

¼ cup (½ stick) unsalted butter, softened

2 cups confectioners' sugar

½ teaspoon maple extract

1. Heat oven to 325°F. Butter an 8-inch round cake pan and line bottom with parchment. Grease bottom of parchment and sides of pan; set aside.

2. Pulse walnuts in a food processor until finely chopped and some pea-sized pieces remain; set aside.

3. In a large bowl, whisk together flour, baking powder, salt, and nutmeg and set aside. In the bowl of an electric mixer fitted with the paddle attachment, beat together ½ cup butter and sugar until smooth. With the mixer on medium speed, add eggs, 1 at a time, beating to incorporate after each addition. Increase speed to medium-high and beat 1 minute more after adding the last egg so the mixture is light and fluffy. Stir in vanilla extract. Blend in the flour mixture just until incorporated. Add the chopped walnuts and stir them in by hand.

4. Spread batter evenly into prepared pan. Bake until a toothpick inserted in the center comes out clean, about 45 minutes. Let cake cool in pan and gently remove.

5. In a clean mixing bowl, beat cream cheese and remaining butter until smooth. Add confectioners' sugar ¼ cup at a time, blending between each addition until smooth. Stir in maple extract.

6. Spread frosting on cooled cake and top with additional walnuts.

butter pecan cake with browned–butter whipped cream

THIS TENDER and rich dessert is the pecan version in my trio of nut cakes. Candied pecans, and a buttery cake are made even more decadent by a cloud of whipped cream laced with nutty brown butter.

You can skip making the candied pecans if you have 2 cups of any type of prepared candied pecans, which you might have around the holidays.

CANDIED PECANS

2 cups pecans, divided

3 tablespoons melted butter

2 tablespoons brown sugar

⅛ teaspoon salt

½ teaspoon vanilla extract

CAKE

1 cup sifted all-purpose flour

½ teaspoon baking powder

½ teaspoon salt

¼ teaspoon ground nutmeg

½ cup (1 stick) unsalted butter, softened

1 cup granulated sugar

3 large eggs

1½ teaspoons vanilla extract

BROWNED-BUTTER WHIPPED CREAM

¼ cup (½ stick) unsalted butter

Pinch of salt

1 cup heavy cream

½ teaspoon vanilla extract

⅓ cup confectioners' sugar

1. Heat oven to 350°F. Line a baking sheet with parchment or silicone baking mat.

2. In a medium-sized bowl, combine pecans, melted butter, brown sugar, salt, and vanilla. Toss to coat pecans. Spread pecans evenly onto baking sheet and bake 5 to 7 minutes, or until toasted. Set aside to cool.

3. Reduce heat to 325°F. Butter an 8-inch round pan and line bottom with parchment. Grease bottom of parchment and sides of pan; set aside.

4. Pulse 1 cup of the candied pecans in a food processor until finely chopped and some pea-sized pieces remain; set aside.

5. In a large bowl, whisk together flour, baking powder, salt, and nutmeg; set aside. In the bowl of an electric mixer fitted with the paddle attachment, beat together the butter and sugar until smooth. With the mixer on medium speed, add eggs, 1 at a time, beating to incorporate after each addition. Increase speed to medium-high and beat 1 minute more after adding the last egg so the mixture is light and fluffy. Stir in vanilla extract. Blend in the flour mixture just until incorporated. Add the chopped candied pecans and stir them in by hand.

6. Spread batter evenly in prepared pan. Top with whole or chopped candied pecans. Bake until a toothpick inserted in the center comes out clean, 45 to 50 minutes. Let cool in pan and gently remove.

7. Make Browned-Butter Whipped Cream: Once cake has cooled, melt ¼ cup butter in a small saucepan over medium-high heat, stirring 3 to 5 minutes. The brown milk solids will sink to the bottom of the pan and turn golden-brown. Pour butter solids into a small bowl or liquid measuring cup, scraping all the browned bits into the cup. Let cool. Carefully pour the liquid butter into another bowl for separate use. Scrape the browned bits into a large mixing bowl with salt, heavy cream, and vanilla. Whip until soft peaks form. Whip in sugar until just mixed.

8. To serve, top cake with dollops of the Browned-Butter Whipped Cream and sprinkle with remaining candied pecans.

MAKES

40 MINI-SANDWICH
COOKIES

HANDS-ON TIME

30 MINUTES

TOTAL TIME

1 HOUR 10 MINUTES

soft gingersnaps with sweet orange cream cheese

MY GREAT-AUNT RUTH always made soft gingersnaps when I was young, so I didn't know traditional gingersnaps were crispy until I was much older. Mom made my aunt's recipe often, which called for an orange-infused cream cheese spread on top. They are ridiculously good! I've made this family classic my own by making the gingersnaps smaller and filling them with my own version of the frosting. The problem is, now that they are small and super cute, I can't help but eat too many!

TARA'S TIP

I have a small cookie scoop that is 2 teaspoons in volume, and I use it here for both the cookies and the filling. If you don't have a cookie scoop, you can measure a cookie to see the size and use it as your guide for the others.

¾ cup unsalted butter, softened

¼ cup canola oil

¼ cup molasses (not blackstrap)

1 cup granulated sugar, plus more for coating cookies

1 large egg

1 teaspoon grated ginger

2¾ cups all-purpose flour

2 teaspoons baking soda

½ teaspoon salt

1 teaspoon ground ginger

1 teaspoon ground cinnamon

1 recipe Sweet Orange Cream Cheese (below)

1. Heat oven to 350°F. In the bowl of an electric mixer fitted with the paddle attachment, beat together butter, oil, molasses, and sugar and beat until light and fluffy, about 3 minutes. Beat in egg and fresh ginger. Add flour, baking soda, salt, ground ginger, and cinnamon. Mix at low speed to combine completely.

2. Roll dough into ¾-inch balls (about 2 teaspoons each) and then roll balls in granulated sugar to coat. Bake in batches on an ungreased baking sheets until edges are crispy and the center is soft but starting to set, 8 to 10 minutes. Cool.

3. When cookies are completely cool, use Sweet Orange Cream Cheese to frost the underside of one cookie with 2 teaspoons filling and sandwich with another cookie. Repeat for all the cookies.

4. Cookies can be stored in an airtight container up to 1 day or refrigerated up to 3 days.

SWEET ORANGE CREAM CHEESE

12 ounces cream cheese, softened

½ teaspoon vanilla extract

½ teaspoon orange zest

½ cup confectioners' sugar

In the bowl of an electric mixer fitted with the paddle attachment, beat cream cheese with vanilla and zest until smooth, about 1 minute. Add confectioners' sugar and beat until smooth.

triple-chocolate layer cake

NOT ONLY IS THIS cake crazy-delicious, but it's surprisingly easy to make as well. For starters, it's a sheet cake. (Honest—I simply cut it into thirds to make a statement cake shape.) The Swiss Meringue Buttercream is a frosting staple, made by dissolving sugar in egg whites and beating to perfection with butter. Use a large piping tip to make the gorgeous poofs (the easiest shape to pipe) and you're done!

MAKES

10 TO 12 SERVINGS

HANDS-ON TIME

25 MINUTES

TOTAL TIME

50 MINUTES
NOT INCLUDING
BUTTERCREAM
PREPARATION

¾ cup packed light brown sugar, divided

⅓ plus ½ cups water, divided

¼ cup Dutch-processed unsweetened cocoa powder, plus more for dusting

2 ounces semi-sweet chocolate, chopped

1½ cups all-purpose flour

½ teaspoon baking powder

1 teaspoon baking soda

½ teaspoon salt

6 tablespoons canola oil or avocado oil

½ cup granulated sugar

2 large eggs

2 teaspoons vanilla extract

1 recipe Swiss Meringue Buttercream, Triple-Chocolate Variation (page 235), prepared

Chocolate curls, if desired

TARA'S TIP

For an easy semi-homemade swap, feel free to use a boxed chocolate cake mix.

1. Heat oven to 350°F. Grease a 10-by-15-inch jellyroll pan and line the bottom with parchment.

2. In small saucepan over medium heat, melt ¼ cup brown sugar, ⅓ cup water, cocoa, and chocolate together. Stir several minutes to combine and completely melt. Mixture will be smooth and look like a thick custard. Set aside to cool.

3. In a large bowl, whisk together the flour, baking powder, baking soda, and salt; set aside. In the bowl of an electric mixer fitted with the whisk attachment, whisk together the oil, granulated sugar, remaining brown sugar, and eggs until well combined, about 1 minute. Add the melted chocolate mixture and whisk to combine. Add ½ cup water and vanilla and mix at low speed.

4. With mixer still set to low, add the flour mixture ¼ cup at a time until just incorporated, then increase mixer speed and beat the mixture 10 to 15 seconds. Transfer batter to pan, smoothing the top to spread evenly.

5. Bake until top springs back when touched and edges are just barely pulling away from the sides of the pan, 15 to 20 minutes. Cool a few minutes, then run a knife around the edges to loosen the cake. Place cooling rack on top of the cake and flip the whole thing to invert the cake onto the cooling rack. Cool completely. Cake can be wrapped tightly in plastic wrap and refrigerated until ready to assemble.

6. Cut cake into 3 (10-by-5-inch) rectangles. Transfer buttercream into 3 piping bags (one for each flavor) fitted with a plain coupler or a ½-inch #806 tip. Place one cake rectangle on a serving platter. Pipe 32 dots (about an inch in size) of the dark chocolate buttercream on the layer, and top with a second cake. Pipe 32 dots of milk chocolate buttercream over the second layer and top with third piece of cake. Pipe 32 dots of white chocolate buttercream on the top.

7. Dust lightly with cocoa powder and serve. Garnish with chocolate curls, if desired.

cherry, anise, and almond crostata

MAKES

6 TO 8 SERVINGS

HANDS-ON TIME

30 MINUTES

TOTAL TIME

2 HOURS
30 MINUTES

SWEET CHERRIES get baked on top of an anise and almond filling for a rustic but utterly delicious dessert. A crostata, or galette, is simply a rustic pie—a filled pastry with folded edges that keep all the goodness in place. They don't need to look perfect; they hold their own with taste!

The almond layer is my take on frangipane—a sweet almond filling with eggs that bakes into a nutty custard. I made frangipane once with anise seeds, and I'm not sure I can ever go back to the original. Those little licorice-tasting seeds are so delicious with the sweet almond.

ANISE ALMOND FILLING

1 cup almonds, sliced or slivered

¾ teaspoon anise seeds

⅓ cup granulated sugar

2 large eggs, divided

1 teaspoon vanilla extract

¼ teaspoon salt

2 tablespoons unsalted butter, softened

CROSTATA

½ recipe All-Butter Double-Crust Pastry (page 198), prepared

2 cups fresh or frozen sweet cherries, pitted and cut in half

2 tablespoons granulated sugar

1 tablespoon fresh lemon juice

Toasted almonds, for garnish

Sweetened whipped cream or ice cream for serving

TARA'S TIP

If using frozen cherries, let them thaw and reserve any juices for another purpose. Toss the cherries with the sugar and lemon juice.

Cherries are a shoo-in for this recipe, but try other fruits depending on the season. Pears are especially lovely with this crostata in the fall.

1. Heat oven to 400°F. Make the filling: In a food processor, combine almonds, anise seeds, sugar, 1 egg, vanilla, and salt. Blend until a paste forms. Add the butter and blend again. Set aside.

2. To make crostata: In a large bowl, toss the cherries with sugar and lemon juice. Set aside.

3. On a sheet of floured parchment, roll out the pastry dough to a 13-inch circle. Transfer dough, while still on parchment, to a rimless cookie sheet.

4. Spread the almond paste onto the pastry circle, leaving a 2-inch border. Scatter or arrange the cherries on top, covering all of the almond paste. Fold the dough up and over the cherries around the edges, pleating the dough as needed.

5. In a small bowl, beat remaining egg with 1 tablespoon water to make an egg wash. Brush crust's edge with egg wash and sprinkle crust generously with extra sugar.

6. Bake until cherries are cooked and juicy, 40 to 45 minutes. If crust starts to get too brown, lightly cover with foil. Remove crostata from oven, cool slightly, and sprinkle with extra almonds. Serve with whipped cream or ice cream if desired.

MAKES

8 TO 12 SERVINGS

HANDS-ON TIME

45 MINUTES

TOTAL TIME

2 HOURS
30 MINUTES

TARA'S TIP

I like to make the cake and frosting a day ahead of time, and then decorate it on the day I'm serving it. If you do the same, wrap the cake layers tightly in plastic wrap and refrigerate until ready to frost. Cold cakes are always easier to layer and work with. Whip chilled frosting to soften before using.

mulling-spice christmas tree cake with cream cheese frosting

THIS CAKE IS MADE with a quintessential spice mixture and apple cider. The texture has a fine crumb, and the spices explode with flavor when paired with molasses and the apple. The combo of spice cake and cream cheese frosting is essential, and decorating this classic with a luster-dusted pine tree forest makes it perfect for the holiday season.

2¼ cups all-purpose flour

1 teaspoon ground cinnamon

½ teaspoon ground cloves

½ teaspoon ground nutmeg

¼ teaspoon ground ginger

½ teaspoon salt

1 cup unsalted butter, softened

1 cup packed light brown sugar

2 large eggs

2 teaspoons orange zest

¾ cup molasses (not blackstrap)

½ teaspoon baking soda

½ cup boiling apple cider

1½ recipe Rich Cream Cheese
  Frosting (page 199)
  (see "Looks Delicious" note)

Sliced almonds

Green luster dusts

Yellow candies, such as mini M&M's

Tootsie Roll candies, cut into small
  pieces for stumps

1. Heat oven to 350°F. Grease 2 (9-inch) round pans and line bottoms with parchment.
2. In a large bowl, whisk together flour, cinnamon, cloves, nutmeg, ginger, and salt; set aside. In the bowl of an electric mixer fitted with the paddle attachment, beat together the butter and sugar until smooth. Add eggs and orange zest and beat on medium-high speed, about 1 minute.
3. In a separate bowl or liquid measuring cup, stir together the molasses, baking soda, and boiling hot apple cider.
4. Starting with the flour mixture, add flour and apple cider mixtures to the mixing bowl alternately in three batches. Begin and end with flour. Mix each addition just until incorporated. Batter will be runny.
5. Divide batter between the pans and bake until a toothpick inserted in the center of the cakes comes out clean, with no crumbs, 25 to 30 minutes.
6. Let cakes cool 15 minutes, then remove from pans and let cool on racks.
7. While cakes cool, toss almonds in a little luster dust to coat and color. Use different green tones of luster dust, if desired, and use a clean, small pastry brush to help coat each almond.
8. When cakes have cooled completely, trim the domed top off each cake so the tops are flat. Place one layer on a serving platter or cake plate. Top with ¾ cup cream cheese frosting and spread to ¼-inch from the edge. Place second layer on top and frost the entire cake with remaining cream cheese frosting. Immediately place almonds and candies on the sides to make Christmas trees.

LOOKS DELICIOUS Edible luster dust can be found at specialty baking stores or ordered online. I used two colors of green luster dust, coloring half the almonds with a darker color and the other half with a lighter color. A clean, small pastry brush can be used to apply the dust.

coconut lime cookies

THIS RECIPE WAS INSPIRED by the crispy coconut cookies from Tate's that I find in the bodegas and stores near my New York City apartment. Tate's Bakeshop started in the Hamptons but has expanded their baked goods to stores across the country. Here I blend the idea of their super light, buttery coconut cookie with my favorite lime sugar cookie. The intense, citrusy lime flavor and a hint of toasty coconut in these cookies is incredible. I'll warn you, though: They are addictive.

MAKES

2 DOZEN COOKIES

HANDS-ON TIME

35 MINUTES

TOTAL TIME

1 HOUR 50 MINUTES

COOKIES

¼ cup fresh lime juice

2 tablespoons lime zest (about 4 large limes), plus more for garnish

¾ cup coconut oil

3 cups all-purpose flour

½ teaspoon cream of tartar

1 teaspoon baking soda

1 teaspoon salt

¾ cup unsalted butter, softened

1 cup granulated sugar

¼ cup confectioners' sugar

½ cup unsweetened, finely shredded coconut, lightly toasted

1 large egg

ICING

2 cups confectioners' sugar

¼ cup fresh lime juice

Crystal sugar, for garnish

> **TARA'S TIP**
> To toast coconut, bake it on a baking sheet in a 350°F oven for 5 to 7 minutes, until light brown in parts. Let cool.

1. Heat oven to 350°F and adjust rack to center position. Line 2 baking sheets with parchment.

2. In a small saucepan over medium-high heat, simmer ¼ cup lime juice until reduced by half, about 4 minutes. Remove from heat and stir in lime zest and coconut oil. Set aside to cool.

3. In a medium bowl, combine flour, cream of tartar, baking soda, and salt; set aside.

4. In the bowl of an electric mixer fitted with the paddle attachment, beat together butter, sugar, ¼ cup confectioners' sugar, coconut, and egg on medium speed, scraping down sides of bowl occasionally, until combined well.

5. Add lime-oil mixture, and mix until combined. Reduce speed to low; add flour mixture and stir until combined.

6. Use a cookie scoop to scoop dough into 1½-inch balls and place, 2 inches apart, on prepared baking sheets. Bake until golden brown around edges, about 13 minutes. Transfer sheet to a wire rack and let cool slightly. Transfer cookies to wire rack and let cool completely.

7. Make icing: Stir together 2 cups confectioners' sugar and ¼ cup lime juice in a small bowl until smooth. Drizzle over cookies; sprinkle with crystal sugar and extra lime zest, if desired. Let cookies rest until icing is set, about 5 minutes, before serving.

MAKES

24 STANDARD
CUPCAKES OR
36 MINI-CUPCAKES

HANDS-ON TIME

30 MINUTES

TOTAL TIME

1 HOUR 15 MINUTES

TARA'S TIP

These vanilla cupcakes are a little different from other cupcakes because they should not brown at all during baking. If you do see that they are browning, they're overdone! These cupcakes will be a beautiful blonde when finished. You'll love their fine crumb and rich taste.

vanilla cupcakes with buttercream frosting

WHEN I WAS A FOOD EDITOR at *Martha Stewart Magazine*, I was tasked with creating a story about piping frosting flowers on cakes. That story is one of my favorites. I was given a month to create and develop the cakes and teach myself the best way to pipe each flower so I could teach the magazine readers to emulate the pictures on the pages.

I spent hours perfecting the petals and leaves of sweet peas, classic roses, cherry blossoms, chrysanthemums, lilies of the valley, and daisies.

These playful cupcakes aren't meant to be the botanical buttercream replicas I made years ago. Just fun inspiration for creating a little happiness on the top of a cupcake. Play with your own designs or copy mine.

3 cups all-purpose flour	4 large eggs
1½ teaspoons baking powder	2 teaspoons vanilla extract
¾ teaspoon salt	1¼ cups whole milk
¾ cup unsalted butter, softened	1 recipe Swiss Meringue Buttercream (page 235)
1½ cups granulated sugar	

1. Heat oven to 350°F. Line 2 standard cupcake tins with paper liners; set aside.
2. In a bowl, whisk together flour, baking powder, and salt; set aside. In the bowl of an electric mixer fitted with the paddle attachment, beat together the butter and sugar until light and fluffy, about 3 minutes. Mix in eggs and vanilla. Scrape down the sides of bowl. Alternately mix in flour mixture and milk in 3 parts, starting and ending with flour.
3. Divide batter among liners; fill standard cups ¾ full and mini cups just below the top. Bake until tops spring back when lightly pressed, about 20 minutes. Cupcakes will stay a light color, so don't wait until they turn golden. Cool completely on racks.
4. Divide Swiss Meringue Buttercream into 5 separate bowls. Divide 1 bowl in half and color one half green for leaves. Transfer green frosting to a piping bag fitted with a #352 notched V tip. Color the other half mustard yellow for the inside of the flowers and transfer to a piping bag fitted with a #10 or #12 plain tip. Color 3 other bowls of buttercream in pink and peach tones, leaving the 5th bowl white. Transfer colored buttercreams to piping bags fitted with couplers and have ready flower tips #3, #80, and #104.
5. Frost each cupcake with the white buttercream. Pipe leaves onto each. Pipe petal flowers and chrysanthemums onto the others.
6. Cupcakes can be stored in the refrigerator until ready to serve.

LOOKS DELICIOUS Piping Instructions: For the petal flowers, pipe 5 or 6 petals onto the iced cupcake using the #104 tip. Pipe a center in the middle. For the chrysanthemums, use the coupler to pipe a ½-inch tall mound in the middle of the cupcake. Use the #80 tip to pipe petals all around, stacking them on top of each other, anchoring onto the mound. Angle the petals up, and make them shorter as you reach the center. Add a small center with a #3 tip.

swiss meringue buttercream with variations

I HAD NEVER TASTED anything but confectioners' sugar buttercream frosting and 7-minute icing until I started my cooking internship after college. It's not an exaggeration to say this silky bit of heaven changed my life. Not only did I fall in love with the texture, the not-too-sweet taste, and the fun method of cooking, but I discovered this buttercream can easily transform into different flavors. And because it pipes like magic, I felt like I was an artist with a new medium to express myself.

There are Swiss and Italian meringue buttercreams. Italian requires a candy thermometer to bring a sugar syrup to temperature. I prefer Swiss because of the easy method of dissolving the sugar in hot egg whites instead.

MAKES

6 CUPS
BUTTERCREAM

HANDS-ON TIME

25 MINUTES

TOTAL TIME

25 MINUTES

7 large egg whites

1½ cups granulated sugar

1 teaspoon vanilla extract

2½ cups unsalted butter, softened and cut into 1-inch pieces

1. In a large saucepan, bring 2 to 3 inches water to a simmer over medium-high heat. In the heatproof bowl of an electric mixer, whisk together egg whites and sugar. Place bowl over the simmering water and continue to whisk vigorously until sugar is dissolved, 3 to 5 minutes. To test, rub the mixture between your fingers—you won't feel any sugar crystals if sugar has dissolved.

2. Transfer bowl to the mixer stand and fit with whisk attachment. Beat on high speed until mixture cools and stiff peaks form, 10 to 12 minutes.

3. Reduce speed to medium-high and add vanilla extract. With mixer running, add softened butter a piece at time. (Buttercream may appear to curdle but will become smooth as you continue to beat it.) The process of adding butter and beating until smooth will take 8 to 10 minutes.

4. Use within a few hours or refrigerate in an airtight container up to a week. Before using, bring refrigerated buttercream to room temperature and beat on low until smooth.

PEANUT BUTTER VARIATION: Follow recipe as outlined above but replace 6 tablespoons butter with ½ cup smooth peanut butter. (I prefer regular peanut butter to natural peanut butter in this recipe.) You'll only need half of this variation for my Decadent Chocolate-Peanut Butter Whoopie Pies (page 201). Freeze extra buttercream for up to 3 months.

TRIPLE-CHOCOLATE VARIATION: Prepare recipe as outlined above. After step 3, divide buttercream evenly among 3 bowls, about 2 cups per bowl; set aside. In separate, microwave-safe bowls, melt 4 ounces each chopped milk chocolate, chopped white chocolate, and chopped bittersweet chocolate on high power in 30-second increments, stirring between each increment. When chocolate is melted, smooth, and cooled, stir into the bowls of buttercream until fully incorporated.

TARA'S TIP

Your butter should not be cold, but not quite at room temperature. Test softness by pressing your thumb gently to the butter; it should hold your print. If the butter is too soft, the buttercream will not come together. If it is too cold, you will have lumps.

ACKNOWLEDGMENTS

—

INDEX

ACKNOWLEDGMENTS

MANY HEARTFELT THANKS go to those who helped make this book happen.

First of all, thanks to my dad, for instilling in me a sense of adventure and appreciation for new things, and to my mom, for her unceasing work, recipe testing, editing, and gracious support.

Thank you to the crew who made this book really shine. Thank you to Ty Mecham for the gorgeous photos, for helping me turn my ideas into stunning reality, and making work so fun. To Veronica Olson for the impeccable prop-styling and artistic eye that brought everything together. Thank you to the ever-cheerful Nancy Kochan and Ayelet Davids who brought the food together and made our days bright. To Susan Vajaranant for being my other food brain, recipe tester, and friend. And to Joyce Sangirardi for the lovely surfaces.

Thank you to my sister Marie for her time and patience with many giant family meals and for her help on photo shoots, and to Kristina Kellett and Ashlee Kennedy for making beautiful things happen at the eleventh hour.

Thanks to my publisher, Shadow Mountain, especially Heidi Gordon, who brought me in with open arms and patiently guided me to the finish, to Lisa Mangum for excellent consideration to the details, and to Heather Ward for the chic and beautiful design.

Thank you to Melissa Griffeths, Krista Teigen, Jade Jones, Jenni Ward, Holly Sander, Emily Mecham, Nancy Hopkins, Jenna Helwig, Janet McCracken, Roma Atkins, and Leslie Kiszka for kindly testing recipes at home so others would have perfect success.

And thanks to Martha Stewart for inspiring me and a generation of homemakers, and to my mentors in work and the food world who gave me the wings to make cooking a profession.

Special thanks and appreciation to Tillamook® for their support and their always-delicious ingredients.

Thank you again to my mom and grandmothers, for showing me the way around the kitchen.

INDEX

References to photographs are in **bold**.